BETTER TOGETHER

HOW 30 DAYS OF SERVICE CHANGED MY LIFE

ALEX QUIAN
GREG WEATHERFORD II

Cover art was created by Angelina Bambina, used
under license from iStock.

First Edition
ISBN: 978-0-578-88199-7

Better Together Foundation
P.O. Box #701022
Dallas, Texas 75370

Learn about the Better Together Foundation
www.allbettertogether.org

Check out the Mentor Moments podcast
www.mymentormoments.org

About the Authors

Alex Quian

Alex Quian grew up in The Colony, Texas, a small suburb of Dallas. He graduated from Cornell University in 2019, where he studied Information Science.

The summer after his senior year of high school, Alex was selected to participate in an entrepreneurial and social impact internship led by Greg Weatherford II, who is now his mentor. What was only supposed to be a three-month internship turned into a transformative four-year learning experience. During this time, Alex had the opportunity to be exposed to and learn from professional experiences such as entrepreneurship, project management, business development, hiring and onboarding, youth development, and much more.

Alex's life was forever changed in spring 2019 when he asked Greg to suggest ways that he could serve his home community. In response, he challenged Alex to complete 30 different service projects in 30 days, and he accepted.

From July 1st to July 31st, 2019, Alex completed 30 different service projects, impacted over 1,800 people, and worked with more than 20 different organizations.

Inspired by this experience, he then went on to co-found the Better Together Foundation, a DFW-based 501(c)(3) nonprofit. Motivated to support the holistic development of youth, Alex spends much of his time creating initiatives and experiential programs to enrich youth in the areas of entrepreneurism, lifelong learning, physical and mental wellness, service-learning, and professionalism.

Examples of initiatives Alex has created include the Let's Thrive Now campaign (launched in April 2020) and the Mentor Moments podcast (launched in September 2020).

Let's Thrive Now was a website where young adults could access valuable, free resources to help them navigate the unique challenges of the COVID-19 pandemic.

Mentor Moments is a podcast launched to provide young adults with the opportunity to learn from executives and leaders who they may otherwise never have had access to, especially with the loss of internship opportunities due to COVID-19.

The podcast has featured executives like Cynt Marshall, CEO of the Dallas Mavericks, Dolf Berle, CEO of Topgolf, Arjun Dugal, CTO of Capital One Financial Services, and more.

If you are interested in contacting Alex, please send an email to alex@allbettertogether.org.

Greg Weatherford II

From a young age, Greg has been inspired to serve his community. In 2002 when he was 12 years old, his love for helping others led him to found his first nonprofit, Young People Who Care. This organization focused on empowering other young people to create service-learning projects and discover the transformative power of giving back. Over six years, the nonprofit completed hundreds of service projects and mobilized thousands of youth across the country to serve their communities.

Greg was fortunate to have his work recognized by groups such as the United States House of Representatives, the Department of Education, Best Buy, Coca-Cola, State Farm, Prudential Financial, America's Promise Alliance, Apple Orthodontics, and the Dallas Mavericks.

Because of Greg's work with Young People Who Care, in 2008 he was selected to The State Farm Youth Advisory Board (SFYAB). This was an innovative philanthropic initiative that allocated $5 million annually to a national board of students to oversee a grantmaking program. Each year, the board evaluated funding requests from nonprofits and issued grants to organizations.

Around this time, Greg realized his experiences launching a nonprofit had given him a love for entrepreneurship and the skills necessary to launch his own company.

After seeking a way to combine his passion for serving the community, helping young people, and entrepreneurship, he created a youth sports and enrichment camp provider called Crestpoint Athletics. Working with municipalities, it became one of the largest youth programming providers in the country and served thousands each summer.

Before turning 30, Greg was able to sell a company. Since then, he spent most of his time volunteering, mentoring young adults, and advising entrepreneurs.

If you are interested in contacting Greg, please send an email to greg@gregweatherford.com.

Dedication

To first responders: thank you for all that you do to protect our communities. We can never appropriately thank you for your dedication and willingness to risk your lives for our health, but your selflessness has not gone unnoticed. You have set an amazing example of strength and courage for us all.

To educators: much like first responders, we have often taken you for granted. This past year has reminded us of the vital role you play in the development of our society. We are grateful for all that you have done and still do to educate the past, current, and future generations.

The Better Together Foundation looks forward to continuing to work with others to champion greater respect, treatment, and support for you all.

To My Mom and Dad

Mom and Dad – you are two of the most caring and hardworking people I know, and you have been my role models for as long as I can remember. I can't overstate my gratitude for the countless sacrifices you've made to create the best possible life for me.

Dad - you have long been my best friend. You were there for many of the formative experiences I had, and you played a huge role in developing the passions I carry to this day. You were always an example of what a good man should be. I am grateful that you showed me the importance of being kind, loving, and dedicated to providing for the ones that matter the most.

Mom - you have always been an inspiration to me. I am proud of all the hard work you did to get to where you are today. I admire how you were dedicated and committed to seeking a better education, growing your career, and building a future for your family. Like dad, you did so much to provide me with the opportunities to pursue whatever hobby or interest I picked up. I will never forget how many times you went out of your way to make sure I could pursue my interests.

Without the both of you, I would not be the man I am today. Thank you again for your unwavering support, love, and selfless sacrifices.

I love you both.

Special Thanks

Countless people have contributed immensely to my learning and growth, and I want to take a moment to thank them.

Thank you, **Dolf Berle** for being the inaugural advisory board member of 30 Days of Service. Your support and insights were invaluable to me as I started my journey, and I cannot thank you enough for your willingness to take a chance on me and for believing in my ability to serve the community.

I also want to thank the rest of the amazing members of the 30 Days of Service advisory board whom I had the great privilege of leaning on. I am eternally grateful for you sharing your time, feedback, expertise, and professional credibility. Thank you, **Nakia Douglas, Zoya Jackson, Catalina Villegas, David Field,** and **Julian Placino.**

I am grateful to work with Alkami Technology, a company that exemplifies leadership in the community. I want to thank **Adrianne Court, Chanel Tyes,** and **Courtney Amigh Mrs**ny - you were among the first sponsors of 30 Days of Service. You all believed in me and my mission, enabling me to embark on a tremendous journey of growth.

To **Kevin Horan** - thank you for being another one of my first supporters. You have always believed in my vision, been a true ally, and served as a role model to me. Your passion for the community and investment in youth development is inspiring. Many thanks to you, Justin, and the rest of the JSX team for all you have done.

To our additional primary sponsors: **the Chris MacFarland Foundation, Blucora, Vari, Andy's Frozen Custard,** and **ARCO/Murray** - thank you for providing valuable resources that helped make 30 Days of Service happen.

To **Myles Kratzer** - thank you for always being a source of help and support for 30 Days of Service and many of our other endeavors. Not only is your creative genius second to none, but you are a sounding board that has constantly helped refine and enhance our ideas!

To **Andrea Williams** - thank you so much for the kind words you shared with me in your interview for Mentor Moments. You reminded me that the work I am doing is impactful, and, frankly, your words were an inspiration in writing this book. I am grateful for the example you set as a leader and all that you do to better communities across the country.

To **Ryan Roberts** - you showed incredible kindness to me when you agreed to document all 30 of our service projects on The CW33's website. Your support was invaluable in spreading the word about the initiative, and I cannot express how grateful I am that you were willing to support me in such a meaningful way.

To **Deborah Ferguson** - thank you for producing a segment on 30 Days of Service for NBC5. I will always remember the passion you showed for my project and am grateful for the light you shined on my work.

To **Vanessa Ramirez** - thank you for allowing me to host many of our service projects at the Boys and Girls Club. Your enthusiasm and coordination were critical to the project's success, so I appreciate you being willing to take a chance on us.

To **Grant Moise** - you have kindly supported my work by sharing it with the world through The Dallas Morning News. You are truly a servant of the community, and I am grateful for the belief you placed in me.

To **Bianca Montes** - since 30 Days of Service, you have often given my work a platform to be shared with the Dallas-Fort Worth community. I cannot thank you enough for helping me inspire others to serve the community.

To **Mrs. Alma Rutledge** - thank you for being the reason this journey began in the first place. I know you advocated for me to take part in the internship with Greg that ultimately led to this project. So, thank you for believing in me and supporting me to go on this incredible journey.

To **Dr. Harris** - thank you for being a source of wisdom and encouragement! You inspire me to be a better servant to the community and a leader.

To everyone who has supported my work and been constant sources of encouragement, thank you! Your kindness will always be appreciated. Thank you, Patti, **Estelle, Stephanie, Greg, Deja, Erin, B, Reika, Reem,** and **Vivian.**

Special Thanks

To all of the Mentor Moments Season 1 guests - thank you for participating in our inaugural season. I have learned much from you, as have our listeners. I am grateful for the generosity you showed in sharing your time and insights with me. Thank you:

- Bill Cawley
- Ossa Fisher
- Jeff Cheney
- Christiana Yebra
- Benjamin Vann
- Jin-Ya Huang
- Dolf Berle
- Cynt Marshall
- Andrea Williams
- Victor Boschini
- Kevin Horan
- Mandy Price
- Kelvin Smith
- Stephen Bohanon
- Dr. Sejal Hathi
- Grant Moise
- Carla Rosenberg
- Faye Iosotaluno
- Arjun Dugal

To countless others - thank you for what you have done to contribute to my growth and the development of our work.

COVID-19 Disclaimer

The vast majority of the experiences detailed in this book occurred between May 2016 and January 2020. Because of this time frame, some of the advice predates the realities of the COVID-19 pandemic.

When applicable, please make sure to adhere to all health and safety guidelines if you choose to follow any advice outlined in this book.

For comprehensive information and resources regarding the COVID-19 pandemic, please visit the following websites:

- www.coronavirus.gov
- www.cdc.gov
- www.coronavirus.jhu.edu

Table of Contents

How to Maximize This Book

Over the past four years, I have gone on a journey that has changed my life. It has allowed me to grow tremendously as a person, student, professional, and entrepreneur.

In this book, you'll receive the highlights of lessons that I've learned along the way. That includes best practices for maximizing your college career, completing service projects, and succeeding as a professional, among other topics.

But before going any further, Let me show you some quick tips on how you can get the most out of this book.

#1: Keep an Open Mind

I've grown so much because I allowed myself to be receptive to new ideas, experiences, and people. If we want to grow, it's essential for us to keep an open mind about experiences, perspectives, and people that may be different from what's familiar to us or what we're comfortable with.

As you read this book, please reflect on how you can open yourself to new experiences, whether they are similar to the ones I have had or completely different.

#2: Have a Pen and Notebook

I want you to take the lessons I share and apply them to your own life. As you are reading, I encourage you to write down lessons, tips, or other insights that you find useful. Write down paragraphs that really speak to you, then think about them and revisit them later. The act of writing instead of highlighting will facilitate you learning, retaining, and acting upon the knowledge you gain.

#3: Challenge What You Believe

Another important part of growth is challenging what you believe. I think many people become scared and defensive when their beliefs are challenged, but I'm here to tell you that it is okay to have them questioned.

If we start to doubt a belief we hold, we shouldn't be afraid. We should explore those doubts. If someone questions one of our beliefs, we shouldn't immediately shut ourselves off to what they're saying - we should try to see their side. Through this process, we may learn that our past beliefs aren't right for us and adopt new and better ones.

On the other hand, we may become more confident in the beliefs we have. Either way, facing and examining challenges to our beliefs enables us to learn more about ourselves and how we view the world. That is what growth looks like.

#4: Seek Out New Knowledge

Seeking more knowledge is essential to further your journey. To grow and be successful, we need to constantly seek out new knowledge. We should never stop learning.

Read books like this one, try new experiences, take courses to learn a new skill, watch documentaries, and participate in other activities that expose you to the world, people, skills, and cultures. We have no excuse - there is more knowledge out there than we can ever know, so there's always room to learn more! Be a life-long learner.

Now that you are equipped to make the most out of this book, I am excited to share with you the experiences that have changed my life.

Introduction

There are a number of significant challenges we face today. Political divides feel deeper and more irreparable than ever. Meanwhile, the progress made towards racial and gender equality seems to have slid backwards, and the wealth gap only continues to widen. This is on top of other issues such as climate change, the opioid crisis, and the global pandemic.

When thinking about these issues that feel insurmountable, it's understandable that many feel like nothing they do can make a difference. For the longest time, I felt this way. I suffered from an induced apathy that affects many of us. My mindset was simply, "I'll be a good person, I'll help how I can, but I'm not going to worry about those problems. Surely, they will fix themselves eventually."

Can you blame me, or anybody else, for feeling that way? I was a 21-year-old kid; what was I going to do about any of these problems or the others that face communities? I did not have billions of dollars to give away, I was not an elected official, and I was not a CEO.

Seriously, what power did I have to make a difference?

Over the last few years, I've learned that I was completely wrong! There are ways that we all can have a true impact.

Introduction

I realized that to create positive change, you don't have to be a senator, CEO, President, or even a student government leader. We can make a difference by being better people, being better to our communities, and being better examples to others. By just doing that, we can be part of the solution to the many problems facing us today, and hopefully inspire others to do the same.

In this book, I will share my story about how unexpected experiences changed my mindset and galvanized me to help others. While reading, you'll see how I went from sitting on the sidelines to leading an initiative that completed 30 different service projects in 30 days, starting a nonprofit, and encouraging others to give back.

Now, I want to share what I've learned with you. I want to shout out my experiences from the rooftops to inspire you to feel empowered to make a difference.

This is the story of how 30 days of service changed my life.

Chapter 1
All Figured Out...
or so I Thought

A Traditional Mindset

I think it's important to start this story at the beginning. For most of my life, I was only concerned about my own success. I thought the universal key to living a fulfilling life was having a great professional career. To me, accomplishing that meant putting all my efforts towards excelling in school and landing a phenomenal job after college.

I was in middle school when I decided to follow this mindset. From then on, I prioritized doing everything I could to be accepted into a prestigious school. I took every advanced class available, went above and beyond on assignments, and became more involved with extracurriculars.

An essential part of that strategy was serving the community because I knew it was something that colleges look upon favorably. I am ashamed to admit it now, but growing up, my interest in service was only to the extent that it served this goal. I mainly did it to check the box.

Not to excuse my attitude towards service, but I justified it through my career-focused mindset. I had convinced myself that I couldn't help anyone until I accomplished my goals.

I found myself reinforcing these thoughts whenever I did serve. I would always leave service projects feeling like I hadn't made any real difference. If I packed meals at a food pantry for three hours, it might have helped the organization get food in the hands of people who needed it that day. But would that stop those same people from having to come back for more food in the future? Because of that, I felt like I wasn't solving the problem.

Since I diminished the impact of my service, I let a feeling of apathy grow. Instead of appreciating the opportunity to help others, I led myself into the trap of thinking that my efforts were largely pointless.

That was my mindset, and it didn't start to change until my senior year of high school. Going into that year, I was excited about the future. My hard work was paying off because I was in an ideal position to go to a well-respected college. I was in the top ten of my class, an officer in the student council, and president of our National Honor Society.

In summer 2015, my parents took me on a trip to tour colleges, and I visited Cornell University. Beyond what I had learned from their unofficial mascot (the character Andy Bernard from The Office), I knew nothing about the school. However, after visiting the campus, I knew for certain that I wanted to go there. It was exactly like the picturesque colleges you see in the movies: historic buildings, ivy hanging off the walls, beautiful quads with students studying on the lawns, and massive, fancy libraries. Not to mention it advertised a plethora of majors to choose from.

Overall, it seemed like the perfect place to learn and prepare for my future career.

QUICK TIP

If you're a high school student heading to college, make sure you take time to research your options. There are a number of factors you should consider. Of course, look at things like tuition, the majors, student-to-faculty ratio, and student diversity. But don't forget to also consider non-academic factors like housing, the climate, and how far it is from home. Remember, you're picking a new place to live as much as you're picking a place to learn. For detailed information on colleges, you can check out websites like College Navigator and US News.

In December 2015, I was accepted into Cornell and as far as I was concerned, my future was secured. The path ahead of me was clear - or so I thought.

Five months later, in May 2016, I was a few weeks away from graduating high school. I figured it would be a good idea to work a summer job, so I whipped together a resume and started searching. Initially, I figured I'd just get a job working retail or something similar, but I happened to stumble upon an internship that immediately caught my eye.

The post read, "Summer Entrepreneur Internship; hands-on experience creating for-profit and nonprofit projects; work alongside other interns; $10 per hour." That sounded like a wonderful learning opportunity, and if I could make $10 per hour doing it, I figured why not? So, I sent off my application.

I soon found myself in a unique internship experience. It delivered what the advertisement promised: for two and a half months, I had the opportunity to help start and lead a variety of different businesses. As someone whose career goals only involved following a traditional professional path within a company, this was an entirely new experience. I found myself unexpectedly enjoying it!

Even more surprising were the positive service experiences I had during the internship. As part of the program, we were responsible for completing a few service projects. Frankly, I didn't have high expectations. I assumed I would carry the same nonchalant attitude towards these acts of service, but I became invested in these opportunities to serve.

One memory that sticks out to me is when our boss brought in ingredients and materials to make peanut butter jelly sandwiches and lunch bags. He told us that today, our one job was to assemble as many sandwiches and bags as we could. We were going to compete against each other, but we couldn't be sloppy either, so it was up to us to find the right balance of working quickly but carefully.

I would never have guessed that I would be into competitive sandwich-making, but apparently, I have that spirit in me because I transformed into a well-oiled machine. About 20 or 30 sandwiches later, we stopped, piled into a car, and headed downtown. Together, we handed out our lunch bags to people experiencing homelessness.

The moment that cemented this experience in my mind was the gratitude we saw from those we served. I remember how they thanked us as we handed them the lunch bags. These were merely lunches, but at that moment, it felt like we were handing out gold.

Although this service project was not all that different from the countless times I served at a food pantry, it felt different. It deeply affected me. I felt a drive to keep giving back to my community like never before.

This experience made me wonder: had I been approaching service with the wrong mindset this whole time? Was giving back something that I want to significantly integrate into my life? Did I need to change my plans for the future?

These were uncomfortable questions to consider, and I didn't take the time to explore them further. College was right around the corner, and I was looking forward to continuing my academic career. So, as the internship came to an end, I did my best to push those questions aside and get ready to head off to school.

Off to Ithaca
In August 2016, I arrived at Cornell University and began a much-anticipated chapter of my life. I was the kind of kid that was eager to be an adult, so this was exhilarating.

One of the first surprises of my college experience was how open students were to engage with strangers. Maybe it's the fact that everyone is in the same boat.

We had all been dropped off in a new place where few of us knew each other, and everyone had the opportunity to build entirely new friendships. Regardless, I was thankful for this openness because after high school, I was looking forward to making new friends and leaving the bubble I had lived in all my life.

Thankfully, connecting with interesting people wasn't hard to do at a place as diverse as Cornell. I swiftly found myself making friends from all over the world. Shortly after I arrived, I was already being exposed to perspectives that I had never seen in my hometown, something that I am still grateful for to this day. In all honesty, the privilege of having such a diverse group of friends allowed me to learn as much outside the classroom as in it.

On a related note, one of my favorite parts about the college experience is the opportunity and freedom to explore many different things. This applies to majors and other areas of interest such as student organizations, hobbies, friends, and experiences.

If you take advantage of this freedom, you will be surprised with how your knowledge and areas of interest will grow and evolve over four years. Prime example: at first, I wanted to be a Government major, but after changing my mind ten times in as many weeks, I landed on Information Science. Even though both of my parents work in tech, I never thought I would work in that industry. However, I enrolled in a coding class and was so intrigued that I knew I had to major in this field.

This goes to show why it's important to try new things and explore. I would've missed out on this major if I hadn't taken a chance and explored a new class.

After establishing my major, I took it upon myself to try every student organization I could find, even if it seemed like it wouldn't interest me. By now, I was embracing my "you never know until you try" philosophy.

One of the student organizations I joined was the Cornell Concert Commission. This group helps organize all concerts that come to Cornell. Our responsibilities included selecting and promoting the artist, building the stage, and working security backstage.

On concert days, we would show up at 7 am and spend the next 20 hours working on our feet. Even though concert days were physically draining, it was easy to forget because it was also so much fun.

To this day I can't tell you what compelled me to join this organization, but being a part of it gave me many of my best memories and friends from my time at Cornell!

You owe it to yourself to get out of your comfort zone. This is true regardless of where you are in life, but especially if you decide to go to college. It's one of the few times in your life where you'll be offered the chance to explore and learn about yourself.

QUICK TIP

For High School and College Students, there are plenty of available resources to learn about different student organizations, classes, and experiences. If you're not sure how to find an organization, you can visit your student affairs office or search on your school's website. If you want to know what different classes your school has to offer, speak with a counselor. And of course, ask your peers. Chances are they've been a part of an organization or taken a class that they enjoyed and can recommend some unique experiences for you to try.

During this time, I stayed in touch with my boss from the summer internship, Greg. I now considered him a mentor, and in spring 2017, I started another internship with him. This internship allowed me to work on new, interesting projects and build upon the skills I gained over the summer.

At first, it was a challenge to balance school, extracurriculars, and my new job, but once I felt I had a handle on it, I found myself enjoying the work even more than I had before.

QUICK TIP

If you feel overwhelmed with your workload, one of the best tools to help you stay organized is a to-do list. This helps you know exactly what you need to accomplish and when you need to finish it. In turn, you can better plan and manage your workload.

This new opportunity gave me even more exposure to what it is like to be an entrepreneur. Some of the work I was doing related to executing community impact initiatives, which I found especially engaging. This was my initial foray into planning service projects, and I found it very enjoyable.

Like the experience I had over the previous summer, I felt a passion for the service I was doing. Soon enough, those initial questions of uncertainty around my attitude towards service and the ramifications it may have on my future began to reappear.

This time, though, I couldn't push the questions out of my mind. Part of this was because I was immersed in social impact work daily through my internship. The other part of it was because of the diverse perspectives I had encountered at Cornell. I had succeeded in leaving my suburban bubble, and it exposed me to numerous social and humanitarian issues I had never really thought about. I frequently found myself having conversations with students from underserved backgrounds who accomplished incredible things because of stellar community programs. These were constant examples of the real impact that service can have.

By the end of my first year, I was sure that whatever I ended up doing professionally, I wanted community impact to be an integral part of it.

While it may seem like my new mindset provided me with more clarity, in truth, it had the opposite effect. I felt confused.

This mindset did not fit into the plan I had conceived for myself. What did that mean for my future? Would I have to give up my professional pursuits to focus on service? What would serving the community even look like? It seemed like I had some huge decisions to make quickly, and that was frightening.

I did my best to forget those feelings of fear and try to find a solution. I needed to understand what making a positive impact in the community would look like for me.

This ended up being a long search. It wasn't until a few years later, in spring 2019, that I started the journey that finally revealed answer.

It was my junior spring, and I had secured a new summer internship in Dallas. Unlike prior summers, I wanted to do more than just work. I felt like I needed to do something that directly benefited my community. I shared these thoughts with Greg, who has always been a thought leader in social impact. I merely expected to receive some recommendations of impactful nonprofits I could serve with over the summer, but little did I know he was going to challenge me to start a project that would change my life forever.

Chapter 1 Reflection Questions

After reading Chapter 1, carefully reflect on and provide responses to the following questions.

When you think of community service, what thoughts or feelings come to mind?

Throughout your life, have you participated in community service? What effect has that participation had on you?

Do you believe that the service of one person can make an impact on solving pressing issues? Explain.

Chapter 2
Stepping Out of My Comfort Zone

An Ambitious Idea

So, what exactly did Greg challenge me to do? He challenged me to complete 30 different service projects in 30 days.

Try to imagine my astonishment when he shared this idea with me. I was expecting him to tell me a million other, more traditional ideas. You know, something like "volunteer at a soup kitchen," or "help out at a youth organization once a week." But no, he challenged me to do one service project, every day, for 30 days straight – all while working a full-time internship.

At first, I did not think he was serious. Although he's a funny guy, he wasn't joking this time.

Naturally, my first reaction was to tell him that his proposal was insane. But I did hear him out, and it sounded less crazy as soon as Greg expanded on his idea. He felt that because I had never experienced true community service, I would benefit from completing so many diverse projects. It would be an effective way to learn about the challenges facing many in my community and how I could have a meaningful impact.

More importantly, he believed that if I went on a journey to complete this challenge, I would be giving others practical examples of how they could serve their own communities. He knew there were plenty of people out there that had a desire to serve but had no idea how to get started. Maybe if they could see me serving, it would be the spark needed to motivate them, in turn.

After hearing more about his idea, I now loved it. But almost instantly, self-doubt crept in. I thought that this was going to be impossible to achieve. I had no idea how I would execute something like this. I knew almost nothing about serving my community! What qualifications did I have to embark on this journey? And even though I genuinely did want to serve, did I want to serve that much? I mean, 30 days of service is a lot.

With these thoughts swirling in my head, my apprehension began to snowball. This led me to decide that I was going to politely decline his challenge and just do one or two much smaller service projects instead.

I met with Greg to let him know that although I liked his idea, I didn't feel like I could do it. It was simply too much. But rather than take no for an answer, Greg encouraged me to reconsider. He told me that even though I lacked experience in this area, he believed I had the requisite skills and drive to get it done. Additionally, he even offered to provide whatever support he could to the project.

I wasn't expecting him to extend that courtesy, and it turned my apprehension into cautious excitement.

Maybe I could do this! It would be hard, but as I learned throughout my time in college, why not go for the unknown? Why not commit to doing something to help my community?

With this newfound belief in myself, I accepted the challenge and fully committed to completing 30 different projects in 30 days.

FRIENDLY REMINDER

Just like me, there will be times where you sell yourself and your abilities short. If you have an idea but think you can't do it, I encourage you to not listen to your doubts right away. Sometimes, we doubt something for a logical reason, but more commonly, it's heavily influenced by our emotions. Moving forward, don't be afraid to take a chance on yourself and try to accomplish your ideas, even if you're not sure what the outcome will be. You may be surprised, and even if you fail, hopefully you will have learned and grown from the experience. While sometimes there can be things to lose, there can often be a lot more to gain.

By the way, this illustrates the importance of having a mentor. A great mentor will embolden you to do things that you see as impossible. They can literally change the trajectory of your life.

To that point, I want to talk about Greg, because without his mentorship, I would not have been able to go on this journey.

Going on this journey of community service was uncharted territory for me, but not for Greg.

He's been a pioneer in this space for a long time. He started his first nonprofit at the age of 12, and over the following 6 years, Greg grew that organization to mobilize thousands of young people across the country to serve their communities.

During his senior year of high school alone, he planned and led two service projects a week, completing a total of 80 by the time of his graduation. So, although 30 projects seemed like a colossal effort to me, I felt optimistic knowing I had an expert to lean on.

The very first task I had to tackle was figuring out what to even call this project. I spent days racking my brain trying to think of a catchy name that would embody the mission of this whole endeavor. I came up with nothing that I loved, but then I realized that the work should speak for itself. The name should be "30 Days of Service!"

And so, this initiative was officially born in April 2019.

We set the program to run from July 1st to July 30th, 2019, so we had less than 90 days to get everything planned. Our work was cut out for us, so it was go time.

The Planning Begins

You may already be thinking, how do you start planning something of this magnitude? You're not alone - that was my thought exactly. With 30 projects to plan, it seemed like there was an infinite number of ways to get started, and an endless number of factors to consider.

With an idea or project that feels too massive to get a grip on, I recommend you start by defining the intended purpose. Clearly defining your purpose will help set the foundation for the other decisions you will make. It becomes easier to make those decisions because you just need to ask yourself: does the choice I'm making tie back into the purpose?

After more thought, the purpose behind 30 Days of Service became obvious. First, I wanted to expand my knowledge about serving my community; second, I wanted to inspire other young people to give back to their communities; and lastly, I wanted to provide examples of ways to serve. By accomplishing these goals, I hoped to have a lasting impact.

Now that I wrapped my mind around the project's purpose, it was easier to start thinking about everything in the context of what would best achieve these goals - starting with the projects themselves.

At this point, I was over my fear of having to identify, plan, and execute 30 different projects. I was now embracing the number of projects as an opportunity rather than an obstacle. I truly felt this way for a few different reasons.

One, completing 30 projects meant I could provide a varied set of examples to people interested in serving. Hopefully, the odds were favorable that at least one project would speak to someone's interests.

Two, it afforded the opportunity to provide examples of both simple and complex service projects.

This was a critical objective because we thought sometimes, people think small projects are not impactful. If that's all someone has time to do, then they may choose to not serve because they feel their contributions won't make a significant difference in the grand scheme of things.

Since I used to think the same way, I don't fault people for having that mindset. However, this is a huge misconception. Progress is often accomplished by small, persistent efforts done by many people that together make a collective impact. I wanted to demonstrate this through 30 Days of Service by completing both small and large projects and showing their impacts. That way, everyone could find examples of projects they could do regardless of their individual capacity to serve.

With this philosophy in mind, it was time to begin selecting the actual projects. I started by thinking about what causes mattered to me the most. I felt this would give me a good starting point and allow me to explore my areas of passion further. These areas were hunger, youth development, and education.

After that, I took some time to research issues prevalent in the DFW community. I spent a lot of time reading articles and having conversations with leaders who were already doing important work in the community space.

In the end, we had a comprehensive list of causes that we felt would fit the criteria we set. This list included causes such as veteran appreciation, voter registration, childhood literacy, and homelessness, to name a few.

Using the list of causes, we then started to brainstorm and research ideas for potential service projects. For every idea we considered, we evaluated it against a few key questions such as, "Can this be done in a day?"; "What community impacts or benefits would it have?"; and "Can this be done for less than $200?"

All in all, we considered well over 300 different projects and ended up with a list of about 60. Whittling our list down to the final 30 soon proved to be even more difficult than going from 300 to 60 ideas.

QUICK TIP

If you're looking for ways to serve, you don't have to come up with service project ideas all on your own! There are a lot of online articles and lists that detail different ways you can help your community. You can even go to the websites of nonprofits in your community, and they will probably have ways you can get involved.

To make sure we stayed true to our vision while finalizing our project list, we created a system to evaluate the projects.

For each idea, we categorized it by the cause it addressed and its requirements (considering factors like how much planning was needed, how much money would be needed, and how many volunteers it would require). With this system, we had a tangible way to directly compare projects and make well-informed decisions.

Finally, after working through each idea (and having a few passionate debates), we selected our list of 30 projects.

However, I'll be the first to admit that list did change several times leading up to, and even during, the 30 days.

Oftentimes, we would have to alter a project idea because we later learned it wasn't feasible or a project collaborator fell through. Sometimes, we had to change directions because of poor planning.

The first time we had to change a project, it was frustrating. But what helped me overcome that feeling was remembering why I was doing this initiative. I was trying to help people, so if something had to be changed to accomplish that purpose, then it was worth it. Whenever you do a project, you have to be ready to accept and adapt to changes because they will inevitably happen.

FRIENDLY REMINDER

You'll see this was one of many times I faced setbacks during this project. But I've learned that setbacks can be positive experiences, too. It's important to stay positive and make sure setbacks don't derail you from achieving the purpose you set. Any time you are facing a possible roadblock, I encourage you to focus, put your head down, and push forward. A setback is only negative if you don't grow from it. Keep moving forward - you've got this!

As I reflect back on this part of the project, I'm thankful to have encountered these speedbumps. They made me develop my ability to be adaptable and flexible, a skill I would need to make it through the 30 days.

Now that I was armed with a plan for the projects I was going to complete, it was time to start getting the support of others.

Securing Community Support

I was fortunate to know that I would be receiving help from my mentor throughout this journey, but in order to succeed and accomplish the goals I set, I would need support from others as well. That meant securing donations, but it also meant finding people I could lean on for emotional support. Completing 30 service projects in 30 days was going to be a draining task, so I felt no shame in knowing I was going to need others to help me stay in the right headspace.

When I returned home from school at the end of May 2019, it was time to start securing supporters. Naturally, I started by talking to my parents about my summer plans. One night after dinner, I sat them down and gave them a PowerPoint presentation about the whole idea.

The first few questions they asked me were, "Are you crazy?" and, "Who are you and what have you done with our son?" I didn't take it personally - after all, I was asking myself the same sort of questions a month ago. I told them that I was aware this would be hard on me and it likely meant I wouldn't be able to see them as much as expected over the summer break.

I also told them how excited I was to go on this journey, and I needed one thing from them: their complete support. And like always, that's exactly what they gave me. From that night on, they took an interest in what I was doing, asking plenty of questions and making sure to check in on me. At times, my parents may not have fully understood what I was doing or why, but what matters is they made sure to encourage me nonetheless. Their encouragement is exactly what I needed to have the energy and willpower to keep pushing forward, even at the hardest moments.

Moving forward, if you're about to embark on an intensive journey, make sure that you ask the people who you trust and care about to support you. In most cases, they will be happy to do so. This will create a support network that can better equip you to face whatever challenges lie ahead.

Having gained the support of my parents, it was time to start bringing in outside help. I needed people that could lend their time, knowledge, or money to develop this initiative.

Our first step was to create an advisory board for the project. This was the best place to start because even though I had already learned a great deal about serving the community from my research and my mentor, it was still important to bring in outside perspectives. It was also an opportunity to solicit feedback from an audience before taking 30 Days of Service public. Fortunately, through Greg's connections, I had the privilege of securing meetings with several leaders in the Dallas-Fort Worth area.

QUICK TIP

Trying something new can be intimidating, but never feel like you have to figure out everything on your own. The world is full of people experienced and knowledgeable in a wide variety of subject matters who love to share what they know. So, if you're taking on a new task, search for experts or knowledgeable people and contact them. Don't be afraid to reach out to and learn from their experiences!

The very first meeting was with Dolf Berle, the CEO of the Topgolf Entertainment Group. This meant the top executive of a global company was going to be the first person, outside of my friends and family, to hear me present about 30 Days of Service. Basically, it felt like I was being put straight into the Major Leagues.

I was nervous. But there was no time for that, so I forced myself to push aside whatever nerves I had and focused on clearly communicating the project's vision and goals.

Thankfully, after I finished presenting, Mr. Berle expressed tremendous enthusiasm and support for the project! He asked insightful questions and shared constructive feedback. He even agreed to join our advisory board right on the spot.

I was incredibly encouraged by this first response. I knew there was still much work to be done, but Mr. Berle's reaction to the presentation was an indication that we were on the right track.

Now, we turned our attention to building out the rest of the advisory board. Given the broad scope of 30 Days of Service, I knew we needed to recruit experts in education, community development, finances, nonprofit management, and other pertinent areas to be successful. Identifying these areas was helpful because it aided us in making a list of people we wanted to approach.

From there, we rounded out the rest of the advisory board with leaders such as Nakia Douglas (Executive Director of TRIO and Pre-Collegiate Programs at the University of North Texas at Dallas), Zoya Jackson (Administrator of Minnie's Food Pantry), and more.

With our board of advisors assembled, we gained not only their knowledge and counsel but also a group of advocates who could help us get other much-needed resources.

Next, we focused on raising the funds to execute the projects. As I was preparing to start this process, I felt some hesitancy. Would companies really want to trust a 21-year-old with their money? Although I was encouraged by the fruitful meetings we had with our board members, I started to wonder if those were flukes. But I had already made too much progress to stop now, so I pressed on.

I'm glad I did because I was wrong. It turns out, there were quite a few companies that were very eager to support the work we were proposing.

I soon learned that people love helping young adults. This is doubly true if you're a young person trying to do something positive for your community. As long as you thoughtfully present yourself and your idea, your chance of getting help is better than you might expect.

I sent out well over a hundred emails to various companies and individuals asking for their support. At least 25 meetings came from these emails, and the CEO of one major company even donated immediately. The offers of support we received were heartening, but even when my requests were denied, it was always accompanied by genuine encouragement for what I was doing.

Those who did support us went all in. I want to specifically shout out two companies that, to this day, are still some of our greatest supporters. I believe these companies exemplify the ideals of corporate social responsibility.

The first is JSX, an aviation service company based in Dallas. Following my initial email, I was connected to their Chief Corporate Soul Officer, Kevin Horan. After presenting our initiative to him, he was eager to support our work.

The second is Alkami Technology, a digital banking software company. I met with their Chief Human Resources Officer, Adrianne Court, and several other members of their Human Resources team. As soon as I concluded my presentation, they committed to supporting the project.

It's not my intention to brag by sharing these experiences. I only want to illustrate the positive reception you can receive from people and show you have nothing to lose, even when you do receive a no. This is true whether you're pitching a big service project to a potential donor or representing yourself as a candidate for an internship or job.

That being said, I do want to offer more than platitudes. There was more to my fundraising strategy than presenting myself as a young person with an idea.

We centered our fundraising plan on appealing to companies who shared our commitment to serving the community. We decided on this strategy because we knew that companies would have the ability to donate the funds we needed, and it was much easier to find contact information for companies than individuals.

After identifying our primary fundraising prospects, we came up with sponsorship packages. We could have directly asked for a charitable donation, but we felt that we would be more likely to receive support if we offered ways to recognize companies' contributions. Example benefits for sponsors included showcasing their logo on our website and printed materials and announcing our partnership on social media.

To approach prospects, we knew that we needed a quality email template to get their attention and secure a meeting. We would also need a presentation that could communicate our vision and plans.

I won't go too in-depth here on how to create an effective pitch email or presentation (that will be at the back of the book if you're curious) but I'll share some high-level tips.

For the email, our goal was to keep it short and sweet. This is generally a good idea, but especially so if you're going to be emailing people at the executive level. Remember, leaders receive numerous emails every day and tend to be very busy. If your email is too long, they may avoid reading it altogether.

While keeping it concise, you should remember to include a compelling narrative and declare your intentions. Our email explained the 30 Days of Service idea, emphasized it was led by a college student, highlighted example projects, shared our board of advisors, and stated that we were seeking a donation. This was enough initial information for a recipient to decide if they were interested in exploring more.

We wanted to also avoid making the presentation too long, but it was an opportunity to expand on what we said in the email. So, instead of merely giving a general overview of the project, we talked more about the motivation behind it, our goals, and how we were going to get it done. Then, we went into specifics about what projects we would be doing. Finally, we discussed some of the challenges we foresaw and how we planned to address them.

In particular, this part of the presentation helped us stand out. Many of the prospects we presented to were impressed by the detail of the contingency plans we already considered.

QUICK TIP

When you're trying to persuade someone to support your vision, it is important to make sure they understand it and why you're passionate about it. However, passion alone is not enough to make something successful or get someone to support you. Many people claim to be passionate about things, but don't follow through. When you present your idea, make sure to back it up with plans, reasoning, and research that show you're serious.

Thankfully, as a result of these efforts, we had the privilege of working with quite a few companies over the summer. With funding secured, we now had a plan and the resources to execute it. Next, it was time to start getting the word out about our projects.

Getting the Word Out

Since inspiring other people to serve was a pivotal part of the 30 Days of Service mission, it was critical to share the story.

To accomplish this, we made a list of local media outlets to contact, sent out emails requesting a feature, and anxiously waited for replies.

One of the first replies we received was from an incredibly supportive man named Ryan Roberts. Ryan was the Digital Content Manager for the local CW affiliate in DFW. From the very beginning, he was very encouraging.

Not only did he offer to write an article about our initiative, but he also offered to set up a blog page on their website to cover every single project of 30 Days of Service!

This collaboration with Ryan occurred shortly before we were set to launch 30 Days of Service on July 1st. It was exciting to know that we had a platform to share our passion to serve. It is impossible to overstate how helpful Ryan and The CW33 were to us.

July 1st was rapidly approaching, and long gone were all my previous apprehensions. I was ready to serve!

Chapter 2 Reflection Questions

After reading Chapter 2, carefully reflect on and provide responses to the following questions.

What are areas that you lack confidence in? What are the ways you can improve your confidence in these areas?

Regarding planning and organization, what are aspects you're good at? What are some areas in which you can improve?

What's something you want to accomplish but have avoided working towards? Why have you not pursued it?

Who are people in your circle that you trust to hold you accountable in the pursuit of your goals? How would you like to ask them to hold you accountable?

Chapter 3
A Marathon and a Sprint
All at Once

It's Go Time

I couldn't believe it! It was July 1st, 2019 - the official start date of this marathon of service projects. A desire to serve the community and three months of planning had finally led to this moment.

The night before, I felt a mix of emotions. Strangely enough, stress wasn't one of them. I suppose I felt confident about the planning that had gone into building 30 Days of Service. However, one thought that did cross my mind was, "Would I be able to do this physically?" I had never done anything 30 days in a row, and I started to think about what physical toll this would have. But I quickly brushed aside those negative thoughts because the initiative's mission was bigger than me. It was go time.

And so just like that, my journey of service began.

In this chapter, I will detail every service project I completed. But I promise this won't be a boring recap - I will share how each project was completed and the impact it had. I hope that while reading, you will keep your mind open and possibly be inspired by one or more of these projects!

Doing any one of these projects is a great way to give back to your community and the people around you. To get the most out of this chapter, I recommend you take notes and even write down service ideas you have as they come to you.

COVID-19 Disclaimer
These projects were completed in summer 2019 before COVID-19. Some of these activities may not be safe to do during the pandemic. This is especially true if it involves working with vulnerable populations (like senior citizens). If you're reading this book during the pandemic and want to serve, please make sure you take the appropriate safety precautions.

Project #1: Launching a Summer Reading Program at a Boys and Girls Club

For our very first project, we started a reading program at a local Boys & Girls Club.

We chose to do this project because so many kids experience learning loss during the summer, so we thought it'd be helpful to give underserved youth access to books and encourage them to read throughout their summer break.

When we were brainstorming this project, the first thought that came to mind was the fun and enjoyment of a Scholastic book fair. Creating that sense of excitement around books and reading was important to make this moment a real treat for the kids.

On the day of the reading program launch, we transformed a room at the Boys & Girls Club into our version of a book fair. Then, when the kids came in, I issued them a challenge. If they read a total of 150 minutes over the next few weeks, I would come back later that month to host a pizza and ice cream party for them. The challenge excited them, and they started choosing a book to read as we handed out reading logs for them to track their reading progress.

That was the kickoff to the reading program, and the kids really rose to the challenge. Before the deadline, all of them reached their reading goals (and some had even surpassed them)! So, on July 29th, we delivered on our promise and came back to host their well-earned party.

The kids were elated about the celebration, but what I didn't expect was how enthusiastic they were about the reading itself. I remember many of them proudly waving their reading logs in the air, wanting to show me how many times they read. Many of them had even finished the book we provided and started reading a new one!

I never thought I'd see a room full of kids so happy to *read*, especially not in the middle of the summer when there were other activities they could spend their time doing. Sure, part of that enthusiasm was probably the pizza and ice cream, but I think this project truly inspired some kids to start reading more.

Our very first project also happened to be one of our most ambitious. I'll admit, I originally wanted to start the 30 days by easing into it. I thought we should begin with easier projects and then build up to more complex ones. However, I'm glad we started with this specific project because it was the perfect way to build our momentum. It made me think: if I can handle one of our biggest projects on the very first day, then the rest doesn't seem so daunting.

If you want to do something similar in your community, I'd encourage you to get in touch with a local organization that provides after-school care programs and tell them you want to organize a reading program.

Next, call bookstores in your area. Some of them probably have charitable programs where they will donate books to good causes. Finally, call pizza places around town to see who might be willing to donate pizzas or at least give you a discount.

Throughout all this planning, make sure you check in with the organization you're collaborating with so you know how many kids are involved and any other logistics needed to make this a successful program.

Project #2: Writing to My Congressional Representative

For my second project, I decided to write a letter to my congressional representative on a local community issue that was important to me. I was motivated to do this project because, in recent years, I had noticed what seemed to be an increase in homelessness around Dallas.

This crisis had become so severe that government action was necessary to make systemic improvements. Knowing this, I was compelled to do my part by writing a letter to my congressional representative.

Although I knew I was deeply concerned about supporting the rights and compassionate treatment of DFW citizens who were experiencing homelessness, I wanted to make sure I was informed. I had some questions. What was the data around increasing homelessness in Dallas? If so, why? What could the community be doing to help in this crisis? What could private businesses be doing to help? What could the government? These questions led me to read many articles with informative statistics and explanations about this growing concern.

After researching and learning more about this topic, I decided to start writing. I stated very clearly who I was: a young constituent in my representative's district who was concerned about homelessness. I then explained why I felt this was an urgent issue, how the problem had grown over the past few years, and how it was only going to worsen with rapidly rising housing costs. I then asked my representative to consider taking or supporting actions that could possibly address this crisis. Specifically, I advocated for increased funding for affordable housing and essential wraparound services such as mental health care.

Once my letter was complete, I found the address for my representative and mailed it off.

QUICK TIP

If you are ever considering writing a letter to Congress, there is a helpful website you can use to find the contact information for any Congressperson. To find this, you can visit www.usa.gov/elected-officials.

To my knowledge, nothing has happened as a result of my letter. I didn't even get a reply. However, I'm not disappointed by that result. I did not view this exercise as futile, because it allowed me to learn more about a topic I was passionate about. It was also empowering to use my voice to raise awareness about an issue that mattered to me.

You may be wondering how I can qualify this as a service project. I admit, it's not what you would normally imagine when you think about that phrase, but that was part of the reason I wanted to do a project like this one.

Meaningful service takes many forms. Someone may not have the time, energy, or money to do a reading program, but we all have time to write a letter to our representatives to ask them to take action on an important issue.

Project #3: Completing Acts of Kindness

In the same spirit of showing that service takes many forms, my third project was to express gratitude to people who had always been kind to me. I wanted to show them that it did not go unnoticed by giving each of them a thoughtful gift and a heartfelt note.

I made gifts for 5 people I wanted to thank. Each gift included a batch of cookies from my favorite local bakery, a gift card, and a handwritten thank you note. Then, I hand-delivered these gifts to every person.

I encourage everyone to take the time to do something nice for someone that has helped you. Whether that's a parent, friend, teacher, or someone else, think of ways you can show your gratitude.

I think we often skate through life not taking a moment to appreciate what we have or letting those around us know how much we appreciate them. I am the first to admit that this was an area I needed to improve on, too. So, take a moment to think about how you can thank others. You don't have to do anything expensive or elaborate. A handwritten thank you card can go a long way.

Project #4: Donating Meals to People in Need

For my fourth project, I packed lunch bags and handed them out to people experiencing homelessness in downtown Dallas. Since it was the 4th of July, I thought it would be a wonderful idea to provide a holiday-themed lunch. Our lunch would include hot dogs, chips, cookies, and cold water.

Fortunately, a local Sonic restaurant was kind enough to donate 100 hot dogs for this project. That was a huge help, and I was touched by their generosity.

The morning of the project, I picked up the food warmer full of hot dogs and began assembling the bags.

It's best to do this with friends as it can be a lot of work, but the time passes quickly when you have other hands to help you (I also recommend having a good Spotify playlist). After all the bags had been assembled, I drove downtown to distribute the lunch bags.

This is a simple project that can be very impactful. Where your next meal will come from can be uncertain for people in need, so taking the time to provide a free meal is a significant and meaningful gesture.

To complete this project, simply go to your grocery store to buy lunch bags, pre-packaged food, water, and ingredients for sandwiches. Then you're good to go!

If you want to provide something useful, you can also include a plastic plate, bowl, or plasticware. Putting the items into Ziploc bags is also a good idea. These are all items that can be reused, allowing your efforts to provide even more value beyond that one meal.

One important thing to note: please make sure you are being careful if you do a project like this. You should not inherently fear anyone who is currently experiencing homelessness, but you should be cautious of traveling to unfamiliar areas.

Please make sure you to take appropriate safety precautions. Projects like this are best done with others, including family and friends.

QUICK TIP

Many grocery stores have a budget to donate gift cards to charitable projects. These donations can help you execute projects like this with minimal costs. If you're wanting to do a service project like this, try calling grocery stores in your area (Target in particular is a company usually willing to donate gift cards). Ask to speak to their HR department or a manager. Please note that you may need to be a 501(c)(3) nonprofit to receive this donation. If you're in school, you may be able to utilize their nonprofit status if you have secured permission from your principal, student organization sponsor, etc.

Project #5: Inspecting a Local Playground

Safe playgrounds and kid-friendly play areas are easy to take for granted, but they are vital to a community. Unfortunately, many communities lack these kinds of places, so for my fifth project, I wanted to highlight this issue. I decided to inspect a local playground for any potential dangers that could be fixed to provide a safer environment for kids.

I started by researching guidelines for safe playgrounds. These included obvious things like making sure harmful trash wasn't in the area (like broken glass), but also concerns that could be easily overlooked such as rusted swing chains, peeling or chipped paint, or protruding bolts.

After doing my research, I made a three-page checklist. Then, I found a playground in an underprivileged neighborhood.

I chose this park because I suspected it was less regularly maintained than playgrounds in more affluent areas. On the day of the project, I spent 30 minutes at the playground looking at everything, diligently taking notes, and snapping pictures of any areas of concern.

After I had carefully examined the playground, I checked the city's parks and recreation website to identify who I could share my findings with. I sent them a kind email carefully explaining who I was, what I was doing, and what I found.

If you're going to do this project, I would recommend taking very detailed notes so you can provide helpful information to the right people who can fix these problems.

I would also advise you to thoughtfully share your findings. It's possible that the person you share your notes with may already know of these problems but lack the necessary funds to fix the issues. So, I would encourage you to make it clear that you're sharing what you found to be helpful, not criticize, and if there's anything else you can do to create a safer space for children, you would love to learn more.

Project #6: Donating School Supplies

Since it was July, families, educators, and schools were already starting to gear up for the next school year.

Returning to school inspires mixed feelings in just about everyone, but this is especially true for families who find it difficult to pay for school supplies.

Although this may sound like a relatively trivial problem, a student lacking appropriate school supplies is likely to suffer from lower academic performance, bullying, and an overall lack of confidence that is detrimental to their educational experience.

For my sixth project, I decided to buy and donate school supplies to families in need. I contacted a local organization that runs a school supply drive for children, Dallas Hope Charities, and they gave me with a list of important needs.

With that list in hand, I drove to an office supply store and purchased the much-needed items. I neatly packaged all the supplies in boxes, labeled them, and dropped them off.

If this project sounds interesting to you, you are in luck! It's very easy to do a service project like this one. It's likely your area has organizations and events that are dedicated to providing school supplies to kids in need, so there are plenty of ways to get involved. I encourage you to google "school supply drive," "backpack drive," "school supply donation," and similar keywords in your area.

In case you come up empty in your search, you can call local schools to tell them you would like to donate school supplies. The school will likely be able to help you get your donation into the hands of those who need it most.

Project #7: Planning a Family Appreciation Day
Just like that, we were already closing out the first week of 30 Days of Service.

Honestly, it felt like a blur. I suppose that when you're focused on a task with few breaks, your days swiftly pass. I imagine I would have felt more tired at this point if it weren't for one crucial resource - my parents. As I said before, their support was an integral part to me being able to complete the 30 days successfully.

So again, in the spirit of showing appreciation to those who do so much for us, I couldn't think of a better seventh project than planning a day to show gratitude to my parents.

Their favorite activity is watching movies, so I got tickets to the best theater in our area and treated them to a nice dinner afterward. It was a simple plan, but that was all it had to be. They appreciated the effort.

When you spend all your teenage years acting too cool for your parents and being on your phone, they appreciate any time you share together. So, the best thing you can do to show your parents appreciation is to spend time with them.

This project is perfect for anyone to do. We don't often think about it this way, but your community starts in your home. A happy family contributes to a happy community, so take the time to do something special for those around you. I promise that they'll appreciate it.

Now that I had the first week under my belt, I felt confident about my decision to go on this journey. I had already learned so much, and I was excited for what was to come!

QUICK TIP

If you made the effort to plan something and spend time with someone, you should make the most out of that time! When you next spend time with your parents, friends, or someone else that matters to you, put the phone away. Make the effort to have a great conversation and show the person that you're happy to be there.

Project #8: Organizing a Voter Registration Drive

To kick off the second week of 30 Days of Service, I helped register young voters. Civic engagement is something that has always been important to me, and with us heading into an election year, it made perfect sense to spend one of my service days helping other young people get registered and excited to vote.

The biggest surprise with this project was how little I actually knew about voter registration. Because of this project, I learned the detailed rules about who can help register people to vote and what the official processes were to do so. Before I could help people register, I needed to become a volunteer deputy registrar within my county, which required me to pass an exam. After passing and obtaining my certification, my county election office supplied me with dozens of registration sheets. I was ready to get started.

I planned to set up a registration station somewhere that I thought would have a lot of young people passing through. Naturally, my mind immediately went to a local community college, so I contacted their student affairs department.

I was given permission to set up a table in a common area, and after scheduling a date and time, I began preparing my materials.

On the day of the event, I arrived on campus, set up my table, and sat for a few hours asking people if they were registered as they passed. For those who were interested in registering, I answered questions they had, helped them complete the registration form, collected the forms, and then delivered them to a local election office.

If you're interested in getting people to vote, you don't even have to do as much as I did. You can start by asking everyone in your friend group and family if they're registered. If they're not, help them find the voter registration instructions for their county and encourage them to register.

If you want to do more than that, become informed on the rules for helping other people get registered in your county, or check out any of the voter registration organizations around the country, like "When We All Vote."

Project #9: Providing Breakfast for Seniors

For my ninth project, I served breakfast at my local senior center. As they say, breakfast is the most important meal of the day, so I wanted to help seniors positively start their day!

To make this project happen, I first contacted the local senior center and told them I wanted to do this project. They were happy to reserve their cafeteria.

Once I had confirmation from them, I called local restaurants to ask if they would donate the breakfast. Thankfully, Another Broken Egg was kind enough to fulfill our request.

On the day of the project, I set up a buffet line in the cafeteria and served seniors as they came in. In between serving food, I sat down with them and engaged in conversation.

QUICK TIP

There are plenty of restaurants and other businesses that will be happy to make an in-kind donation (like food, drinks, items) to your service projects. All you have to do is take the initiative to ask! When you call, you should ask to speak to a manager and give a quick explanation about your project and specific request. Generally, your best chance for quickly securing a donation is with locally owned businesses, as national chains may have processes or policies that can make it difficult.

I loved this experience. Everyone was so thankful to have me there, and you could tell that every second of my time was appreciated. Unfortunately, I think many of the seniors rarely received visits, so they were happy to have a young person spend time with them.

The whole experience made me reflect on how little time I spent with my grandparents. All but one of them have already passed away, and I do regret that I didn't make more of an effort to spend time with them.

I encourage you to at least call your grandparents often and have a conversation with them. Although I'm writing this book during the COVID-19 pandemic, I hope you will make time to see them when it is safe to do so.

Just making an effort to spend time with your grandparents is an act of service. But if you feel like serving other senior citizens, then contact a senior center and ask how you can get involved. Whether that is playing games with seniors, bringing a meal, or something else, you will never feel like anyone appreciates your time more than seniors do.

Project #10: Donating Books to a Children's Home

My tenth project was a bit of an improvisation. Like I told you in the previous chapter, not everything worked out according to the plan, and the project originally scheduled for this day was one example of that.

That being said, I'm grateful my initial plan did not work. It gave me the opportunity to create a project directly inspired by the positive service experiences I already had in my first week of service. In this case, that was the reading program we launched on day one.

I loved seeing how overjoyed kids were to receive a free book for the reading program, so I wanted to do a similar project. We still had some books left over, and since I did not want them to go to waste, I thought it'd be a good idea to donate them to a children's home. I knew that sometimes their resources could be limited, so this could help ensure that their kids had plenty of books to read.

I gathered the books we had and picked out some new books, too. It was my goal to get a broader selection because unlike the reading program, I had no idea about the ages of the children who would be reading these books. Once I had a diverse collection, I packed the books into boxes and gave them to a staff member from a local children's home.

If you want to do something like this project, you can take the same route I did of calling a bookstore and asking if they would be willing to donate some books. If you don't want to do that, consider having you and your friends collect books from your homes that you probably won't read and are willing to donate. You can even go to thrift stores, buy discounted books, and donate those.

Regardless of how you acquire your books, I'd recommend making sure you have a varied selection that has something for all ages. If possible, I would recommend trying to collect books that represent diverse ethnic perspectives.

Once you have your books, call a local children's home, Boys & Girls Club, or a similar organization to ask if they would be willing to accept your donation.

Project #11: Planning a Student Leadership Workshop
Since one of the goals of 30 Days of Service was to inspire other young people to serve their community and be leaders in general, it only felt appropriate to spend a day teaching leadership skills to students.

For my eleventh project, I planned and led a workshop on leadership for a group of high school student-athletes. The workshop featured a keynote speaker and activities around topics such as communicating effectively, working together as a team, and more.

Following the instructional portion of the workshop, we all worked together to create meal bags for people experiencing homelessness. I took some inspiration from the project I did during my summer 2016 internship - I grouped everyone into four teams and made it a challenge. The team who could make the most meal bags in 15 minutes while maintaining the highest quality would win. This meant every team had to work together to make peanut butter and jelly sandwiches, package them up, and put them into a bag along with cookies and a water bottle.

This was easily the best part of the night. It was amusing to see the different strategies teams came up with and how competitive everyone became. After 15 minutes had passed, I called time and declared the winning team. Only that team won bragging rights for the night, but everyone had the satisfaction of having an impact. This was probably the most fun they've ever had serving, and I hope it showed them that service projects can be both fulfilling and enjoyable.

As everyone got ready to leave, I gave each student a planner that I custom made, which would help them put everything they had learned into practice.

When I began 30 Days of Service, I thought I was passionate about educating and investing in others, especially young people. This project allowed me to experience that firsthand and affirmed that it is one of my passions! This was just one of the projects that ultimately inspired me to continue serving even beyond 30 Days of Service (that's all I'll say for now, I don't want to get ahead of myself).

Project #12: Hosting a Movie Day at the Boys & Girls Club
For my twelfth project, I returned to the Boys & Girls Club to host a movie day for the kids. Everyone loves going to the theater, munching on buttery popcorn, and enjoying an entertaining movie. And I knew that for many of these kids, going to the movies was a rare treat, so I figured why not bring that experience to them?

Fortunately, the Boys & Girls Club I worked with had a movie room setup. That was a big plus, and it meant all I had to do was bring the snacks and movie.

Before the project, I visited a supermarket and picked up a giant bag of popcorn and other essentials like cookies, juice, napkins, and plates. When I arrived at the club, I set up my small concession stand, created a system to serve the snacks in an orderly way, and switched on the movie.

All in all, it was a straightforward but fun project. The biggest challenge was getting everyone into their seats and calming them down, but once the movie was going, all the kids were quiet and enjoyed their time!

Fast forward an hour and a half later, the movie wrapped up and I hit the lights. As I ushered the kids out, they all thanked me. Overall, I'd say my first theater management experience was a success.

If you have the time to give back, this is an excellent project to do at a local Boys & Girls Club, children's home, or a similar organization. To get started, call a youth organization and ask if they'd be willing to let you come host a movie day.

Once you have their permission, develop a quick plan for your movie day. What movie are you going to watch? What kind of snacks are you going to bring? What are your rules about snacks?

Crucial tip: make sure you have several movie options and methods to watch them. When I went, I realized that their movie room only had a DVD player, and I didn't have DVDs. I had my laptop and tried to play the movie from there, but the wifi signal wasn't strong enough to stream the movie. I had to switch over to my hotspot.

It was not ideal having to figure all of that out on the fly, so make sure you plan ahead and save yourself the headache by checking with the youth organization and having backup options just in case.

Project #13: Writing Letters to People Who Impacted Me
My second week of 30 Days was wrapping up, and it felt like time was passing by rapidly.

When I took a moment to reflect, it was really hard to believe that I had already completed 12 projects. Somehow, I had avoided feeling overwhelmed by this point. I owed that to the mentorship and role models I have had in my life and their strength, which I wanted to emulate as I went on this journey.

In this reflective mood, I felt it was important to make my thirteenth project about telling my role models how grateful I was for what they taught me. So, with that in mind, I got to work writing letters to those who had influenced me.

In each letter, I made sure to write out the specific ways they had impacted my life, what I had learned from them, and how their example was helping me get through this 30 Days of Service challenge.

Then, I mailed the letters off. Project complete!

This was a wonderful opportunity to show people how important they were to me and be thankful for the lessons I had learned from them. I don't want to be too philosophical, but in the "nature vs. nurture" debate, I fall squarely on the nurture side. So, to me, there's nothing more important than the role models in your life and the various experiences you have that shape your mindset and view of the world.

I appreciated having a moment to reflect on the people and experiences that have contributed to who I am. I recommend that you do this project yourself. Even if you choose not to write letters to anyone, it's important to your growth that you recognize the influences in your life.

Project #14: Raising Awareness for and Donating to a Charity

As I said previously, service can take many different forms. Sometimes, the best way you can serve is by shining a light on the work others are doing and donating to support their causes. This is what inspired my fourteenth project, which was to raise awareness about a nonprofit doing meaningful work and make a donation to them.

I began researching nonprofits in the Dallas-Fort Worth area that already had a track record of making a difference. It was also important for me to identify a nonprofit that was smaller so that I could use my platform to amplify their voice. There's nothing wrong with supporting well-established nonprofits, but sometimes it is beneficial to help smaller nonprofits get attention so that their support base can grow, and thus their impact.

Ultimately, I found Rays of Light, a fantastic organization that provides support and relief to families with special needs children. After reading more about this organization, I loved the work they were doing and wanted to spotlight it. I felt they were the perfect nonprofit to spotlight with this project.

I reached out to the nonprofit to make a donation and tell them we wanted to highlight their work. On the day of the project, I posted a short video about Rays of Light on our Instagram and shared information about what they're doing and how others could get involved.

Again, making a difference in your community isn't about doing all of the hard work by yourself. You will often find yourself feeling like you don't have time to serve, and that's okay. However, it's important to know that amplifying the works of others is still service and a great way to have an impact.

If you can afford to, I encourage you to start giving money to a nonprofit that does work you believe in. If you can't afford to, that's okay. Consider sharing some of their posts on social media to get the word out. Maybe someone else will see your post and be directly inspired to help out, and just like that, you will have made a difference with only a few seconds of your time.

That being said, don't think I'm giving you a blank check not to serve! Absolutely advocate for causes and donate to others, but we all have a role to play in building better communities. So, don't forget to still get out there and give back.

Project #15: Participating in National Give Something Away Day

When I originally researched projects for 30 Days of Service, I learned that July 15th is "National Give Something Away Day." And yes, it's exactly what it sounds like.

On this day, people are encouraged to donate things that might be better used or more appreciated by someone else. I loved the idea behind this day, so I knew I wanted it to be my fifteenth project. But I wanted to take it up a notch.

I decided to do this by contacting a company called Atos, who allowed me to expand my reach by hosting a donation drive at their offices so their employees can participate in Give Something Away Day too.

Leading up to the 15th, I worked with the Atos team to create flyers that they would use to promote the donation drive. Then, on the day of the project, I brought a table and some bins to set up in their cafeteria to collect donations. I was only there for an hour, but I was so touched by the outpouring of support we received.

I soon had way more items than I could manage to carry by myself, and I was floored to see that people had donated nice pieces of clothing, accessories, tools, bags, and other items that I knew would make a difference to someone in need.

With my car packed to the gills, I drove to Minnie's Resale Boutique and donated all the items I had collected. (If you're wondering, Minnie's Resale is a store whose sales fund their food pantry, which you'll hear more about in the upcoming projects.)

If you're interested in doing something like this project, then I have good news for you! You don't have to wait until July 15th to participate. I challenge you to look around your house right now and find items you don't use anymore. These can include clothes, accessories, bags, and toys.

Pack these items carefully and donate them to a thrift store. This way, someone in need can have the opportunity to put your item to use.

We often take for granted everything we have and don't realize that for some people, that jacket you hardly ever wear could become their most prized possession.

QUICK TIP

Serving the community is always better with friends! It is an effective way to increase your impact and the fun you have while serving. This project is an easy way to get other people involved. It won't take much of their time, and everyone has at least one thing they can give away. Ask your friends to consider donating something and helping you take the items to a donation center.

Project #16: Hosting an Appreciation Dinner for Veterans

For my sixteenth project, I wanted to give back to the veteran community we have in the Dallas-Fort Worth area.

I have a personal connection to veterans. Several of my extended family members are in the armed services, and in high school, the American Legion sponsored my trip to participate in Boy's State.

If you don't know, Boy's State is a week-long leadership experience hosted by the American Legion. As part of this experience, young men from all over Texas get to participate in a mock government and learn about civics.

Boy's State taught me many valuable lessons and gave me some of my fondest memories, so I was happy to say thank you for being able to participate in the program. That is what prompted me to provide dinner to a local chapter of the American Legion.

I started by contacting the chapter's leader. After explaining 30 Days of Service and what I wanted to do, he helped me coordinate a date and time for the dinner.

From there, I started asking restaurants around the area if they would be willing to donate to this dinner. I called dozens of places and in total, I received enough food for well over 50 people. The dinner included meals donated by Rudy's BBQ, Blue Goose Cantina, Jason's Deli, Macaroni Grill, and Maggiano's - all delicious, by the way.

Shortly before the dinner, I ran around picking up the meals (word to the wise - if you're ever carrying food around, pack used towels or blankets so that you avoid any spills on your seats - trust me on that one). After setting up the buffet, I stayed for their meeting and served food to every veteran.

At the conclusion of the meeting, the chapter leader was kind enough to allow me to say a few words of appreciation to the veterans. He also gave me an American flag pin as a thank you for my time!

This was an inspiring project, and I'm so glad I was able to share time with a group that has done so much for us all.

If you would like to thank the veterans in your community, I recommend you contact some local veterans' organizations. You probably have an American Legion post in your area, but if not, there are likely similar organizations. Reach out and let them know you want to help - it doesn't even have to be an elaborate dinner like I did. It could be as simple as donating some gift cards or bringing some takeout meals to veterans who would appreciate them.

Project #17: Giving Frozen Treats to Youth Athletes

The Texas summer is, as you may expect, absolutely grueling. Playing outside too long without proper hydration can turn into a serious issue quickly, so staying cool and hydrated is essential.

Because of this, I thought it would be nice to bring some frozen treats to kids attending a local summer camp to cool down (note: I'm pretty sure doctors would recommend other ways to keep kids safe in the heat, but hey, it's a nice to do).

First, I had to secure the frozen treats. Thankfully, this was relatively easy because throughout 30 Days of Service, we had the privilege of working with a wonderful company, Andy's Frozen Custard. They are as passionate about serving the community as they are about serving up some of the best custard I've ever had. When I told them about this project, they were happy to participate.

Now that I had secured the treat cups, I got in touch with a local recreation center and asked if I would be allowed to bring the frozen treats to one of their summer camps.

I got the OK and scheduled a date to drop by. On the day of the project, I arrived with my cooler full of custard and handed them out to the many overjoyed kids.

The frozen custard did not last long - even the parents started digging in. By the time I left, there were many happy faces.

This small act of kindness brightened the day of at least 30 strangers, and that is one of the ways you can make your community better.

I would suggest that you think about other random acts of kindness that you can do in your community. It doesn't have to be frozen treats - maybe it's buying the meal for the person behind you. Maybe it's surprising one of your teachers with a gift card. My point is you should do something nice for people without an expectation of getting anything in return. That's the only criteria here - so get creative!

Project #18: Hosting a Life Skills Class

I have been waiting so long to tell you about this project because it was one of my favorites. For my eighteenth project, I returned to the Boys & Girls Club I had been working with and hosted a class about soft skills.

If you're not familiar, Oxford Languages defines soft skills as the personal attributes that enable someone to effectively interact with other people. This includes attributes such as character traits, social intelligence, emotional intelligence, and communication skills.

In my experience, soft skills are important in becoming a successful student, professional, and leader. Despite their importance, soft skills do not receive the attention they deserve in school curriculum.

For example, think about how many math classes you've taken throughout your academic career compared to classes focused on being a better communicator. I'm willing to bet you've taken way more math classes.

Now, I'm not saying that math isn't important - in fact, it is very important - but my point is that because technical skills are often the focus of our education, we usually don't learn soft skills until much later, like in our first jobs.

Although learning on the job can be as effective as learning in the classroom, you also have much less room for error, because you have to face real consequences as you learn. It also means that if you never have experiences that allow you to gain soft skills, you may never learn them at all.

I realized that students from underprivileged backgrounds often miss out on those experiences, creating an additional obstacle for them to overcome in their pursuit of success. For this reason, I wanted to teach a class on soft skills so that at the very least, they gained exposure to what term meant and had some direction on how they could independently grow those skills.

To prepare for this project, I first researched different soft skills that are important in professional settings.

A few skills soon rose to the top: communication, teamwork, time management, and listening. Since this was 30 Days of Service, I added a fifth: service.

I wanted to make this experience as enjoyable and impactful as possible. I knew that standing in front of a classroom lecturing these kids was a quick way to lose their attention, so I had to find another way to deliver the material. I looked up ways to teach these topics through engaging activities and exercises. Once I felt I had an effective curriculum planned out, I created a PowerPoint.

On the day of the class, I was excited to share my curriculum with the students. I opened the class by explaining why I was there and what the goals of our time together were. After all, that is exactly what I would've wanted to know if I was in their position.

Additionally, I wanted to make it clear that this class was an opportunity for them to explore something they probably hadn't learned before, and they were free to ask questions.

It quickly became obvious that everyone was willing to listen and take my visit seriously, which made my job a lot easier. Then, we got into the presentation itself. For each topic, I gave a quick overview and followed it with an exercise to give the students a chance to apply what they had just learned.

This project became one of my favorites because of what one student said to me after the class was over.

As everyone was leaving the classroom, she came up to me and said, "Thank you for coming. Most people don't make the time to come talk to us, and when they do it's never about stuff like this."

She said this with such sincerity. Today meant a lot to her, and I would like to imagine she left that classroom feeling empowered to be successful. This moment moved me so much, and it felt like I made a significant difference that day.

I couldn't guarantee success for these students, but I believed that they genuinely felt invested in and like someone wanted them to succeed. It was an immense privilege to teach that class.

If you're interested in doing something like this project, you should start by contacting a local youth organization. With the help of the organization, create a curriculum for your class. Don't be afraid to draw plenty of inspiration from the internet. You don't have to reinvent the wheel - what matters is showing up and spending the time to help others learn and grow.

Project #19: Volunteering at Minnie's Food Pantry

For my nineteenth project, I volunteered at Minnie's Food Pantry, a Dallas-Fort Worth-based nonprofit that is truly incredible. The organization is led by Cheryl Jackson, and they have served over 14 million meals to people in need across the Dallas-Fort Worth metroplex.

What I love about Minnie's is they do this in a truly unique way. Their goal is not just to provide meals, but to do so in a "red carpet" experience. That means when you come to their food pantry, you're not just picking up cans - you're also having volunteers help you make selections and take them to your car.

As you've seen by now, volunteering's more fun when you do it with friends. So, for this project, I took along a group of interns from two of our sponsors, Alkami Technology and JSX.

I mentioned them in the last chapter, but both companies were so enthusiastic about 30 Days of Service that they wanted to be involved however they could. So, this was an ideal opportunity to bring them along and work together to make a difference.

On the day of, we arrived bright and early at 7:50 am. I made sure to grab breakfast for all the volunteers beforehand, so we all started our shift well-fed and in a great mood.

After a brief orientation from the Minnie's team, we received our assignments and set off to serve. We ran a gamut of tasks. From 8:00 am until about 12:30 pm, we did everything including unloading boxes of food, refilling shelves, moving furniture, sorting items in their Resale Boutique... you name it, I'm sure we did it! It was a lot of work, but it felt great to do. It was especially rewarding knowing we were helping such a wonderful organization.

If you're looking for something fulfilling to do with friends, finding a local nonprofit to volunteer with is always a good option.

QUICK TIP

Planning your own service project can be an incredibly fun and rewarding experience, but there is no shortage of places you can volunteer at like Minnie's Food Pantry. To search for volunteer opportunities in your town, check out websites like www.volunteermatch.org.

Project #20: Organizing a Donation Drive

My next project also involved Minnie's Food Pantry, but this time, I would be donating items. For the twentieth project, I hosted a donation drive outside of a local grocery store and asked for shoppers to purchase items like food or school supplies that I would donate to Minnie's Food Pantry.

Once I had secured permission from a local grocery store, I checked with Minnie's Food Pantry to confirm a list of items they needed. After getting that list, I made simple flyers so that shoppers had an easy checklist to follow once they were in the store.

The day of the project, I sat outside the grocery store for a little over three hours, politely talking to shoppers heading into the store and asking them to participate in the donation drive.

I'm very happy to say that the donation drive was a success!

We were fortunate to receive more donations than I could have anticipated. Many people gave one or two items, but some purchased a whole shopping cart full of items!

By the time I was ready to leave, I had 3 large moving boxes filled to the brims with food and other items. Minnie's Food Pantry appreciated my donation.

I loved this project because it allowed others to easily give and serve the community. Normally, if someone wanted to donate, they would have to spend time finding out what a nonprofit needs, purchase those items, then go out of their way to drop off the items. This project basically cut out the first and third steps to make it as easy as possible to serve, and people responded positively to it.

If you want to donate to a nonprofit, then I encourage you to consider doing a project like this. This is a wonderful way to donate a large number of items without breaking the bank. This is also a way to get more of the community involved in service.

I recommend starting by calling local grocery stores in your area to get permission to set up outside their doors. It is important you make sure you're allowed to be there before you start planning.

Once you get the OK, then you should get in touch with a local nonprofit and see what items they need.

Using this information, make little flyers with the items on them so that way shoppers can have a reminder of what you're interested in collecting. It doesn't have to be anything fancy - it can be something you create in Word, which you can print at home or a printing shop.

Project #21: Volunteering Digitally

For my twenty-first project, I completed digital volunteer projects using Freerice.com and the Charity Miles app. Given the limitations some interested in serving may have, I thought it would be a good idea to show others that you don't even need to leave your house to volunteer.

In a way, I guess this project was a year ahead of its time!

I started by googling "ways to digitally volunteer," and came across articles recommending Freerice.com and Charity Miles. They're both cool concepts. Freerice donates rice to impoverished communities for every typing challenge that you complete on their website. Charity Miles tracks how much you run during workouts and then makes a donation to a charity or cause of your choosing. The more you move, the greater your donation.

On the day of the project, I spent an hour on Freerice.com, and then went for a run. I'll admit that cardio is not my strong suit, but Charity Miles was a great way to donate to a few causes.

Now more than ever, there are plenty of ways to volunteer digitally.

If you are bored or looking to try something new, why don't you google ways to volunteer digitally? Another fun idea is to turn it into a friendly competition and encourage your family, friends, and coworkers to join you.

Project #22: Delivering Bags with Essentials to People Experiencing Homelessness

On the twenty-second day, I decided to do a project benefiting people struggling with homelessness. This time, instead of donating meals, I was going to create care packages with essential items like socks, toiletries, hygiene products, and snacks.

The first step in this project was deciding what items were going to be included. To make this project most effective, I wanted to be intentional with the items we donated. Ideally, the items I purchased could be used multiple times.

The list I came up with included toothpaste, toothbrushes, socks, bath towels, body wash, deodorant, reusable plastic plates and cups, utensils, dental floss, hand sanitizer, and lotion. The plan was to package these items into drawstring bags, which would be another useful item.

I knew that acquiring the supplies was going to be expensive, and I wasn't sure I would have the funds for it. Thankfully, I had a lot of help.

Earlier in the month, I was fortunate enough to partner with a company called Vari, and they were kind enough to allow me to host an onsite donation drive.

Thanks to the generosity of their employees, a significant amount of the items I needed for this project were donated to me. This allowed me to serve even more people than I had originally planned.

With supplies in hand, I got to work. After I made the bags, I drove around downtown handing them out to the first people I saw.

Like the meal bags I donated for my fourth project, this is one way you can help those in need in your community. If you're unsure what to include in your care kits, you can always search online for lists of what items are most useful.

I also want to emphasize again that you should be careful if you are planning a project like this. Please plan carefully and know exactly where you're going. Don't forget it's important to bring a friend, parent, or guardian along with you.

Project #23: Creating a Get Well Soon Kit for a Family Friend

This was another project where I called an audible, but this time it wasn't because plans didn't work out. While working on 30 Days of Service, a friend had to unexpectedly undergo major surgery. Thankfully, everything went well, but it was going to take them some time to recover.

Knowing how tough the recovery process could be, I wanted to put together a little kit to help them get well soon.

My goal was to give them everything they would need to be comfortable and not have to leave the room except for meals.

I purchased essentials like new pillows, blankets, water, and snacks, but also smaller items that might be appreciated like mints and activity books.

Once I had my items, I tried to package them nicely into a basket. I'll tell you that it did not end up looking particularly beautiful. Gift packaging is not a skill of mine, but it's the thought that counts!

With my gift in hand, I went and surprised my friend. She was touched that I took the time to plan this nice gesture, and she later told me that it helped make her recovery a little more tolerable. It felt great to be able to make her feel loved, and all for less than $100.

The next time someone you know gets sick or goes through a medical procedure, consider putting together a package for them. Being under the weather is no fun, so anything you can do is always going to be appreciated. Think about essentials like chicken noodle soup, sports drinks, and snacks. You can also customize the care kit by including activities and items you know they'll love. I promise it will make their day!

Project #24: Showing Appreciation to Educators

I am fortunate to have been taught by some stellar educators in my life. Being an educator is one of the toughest and most underappreciated jobs, so anyone who commits to teaching students should be commended. It was important to me to show educators that their efforts are greatly appreciated, and I decided to say thanks by providing a meal and appreciation gifts to educators.

To organize this event, I worked with a local organization that frequently works with educators. In doing so, I had a partner that could invite educators to attend this event and provide access to a facility to host the lunch.

With this partnership secured, I could now begin to finalize my plan. This included steps like drawing up the room layout, deciding the type of food, and creating the schedule for the event.

In addition to the appreciation gifts, I wanted to give the educators a chance to win a larger prize. I got in touch with Vari again, who makes standing desks and other furniture that is quite popular with educators.

To my surprise, they offered to donate a classroom makeover for four lucky educators. Their continued generosity was inspiring, and I was excited that some educators were going to leave the event with this marvelous gift. I also received gift cards from Kenny's Restaurant Group, who provided enough for every educator. Thanks to them, no one was going to leave empty-handed.

With all of the components in place, the day of the event was perfect. It was a privilege to give back to individuals who contribute so much to our communities.

If you can, I would encourage you to plan something similar for educators in your area. You can serve educators from your school or an organization like Teach for America.

If you don't feel up for the task of planning an event, that's completely okay! You can do something as simple as bringing breakfast or lunch to educators that you know or giving gift cards with a handwritten note.

Any gesture will be appreciated and make their day. I think serving educators is one of the most fulfilling acts of service you can do, so please give it a try some time!

Project #25: Helping a Neighbor in Need

Like the Get Well Soon Kit, this project was inspired by something that happened during 30 Days of Service. While serving, I learned that one of my neighbors was experiencing a stressful and time-consuming situation.

Although I could not alleviate the situation itself, I still wanted to help. I thought the best thing I could do was help them in other ways. My hope was to take errands off their plate so they could focus their attention on their situation. So, for my twenty-fifth project, I offered to help my neighbor.

I still remember the shock on their face when I told them I wanted to help. Understandably, I don't think they were used to someone asking for more chores to do! With a laundry list of items, I spent the better part of the day running errands for my neighbor, which was a rewarding experience.

I had already learned this lesson earlier in my service journey, but this day reminded me that making a difference within a community begins with the people closest to you - yourself, your family, and your neighbors.

My offer to help my neighbor gave them some much-needed positivity during a difficult time, and that's what I feel is an important part of service: spreading positivity.

Moving forward, look for ways that you can help those in your neighborhood. Whether that's getting groceries for an elderly person, mowing someone's lawn for free, or something else, spread some positivity by donating your time to someone who will appreciate it. It will be more than worth it.

QUICK TIP

If you like the idea of helping your neighbors but don't know where to start, you can always try to go to social media. Reading posts in community groups on Facebook or on apps like Nextdoor can be effective ways to learn about opportunities to help others in your neighborhood or community. Like any other time you are going online, make sure that you are being safe and mindful. If you're a minor, make sure you do this with the help of a parent or guardian.

Project #26: Donating New Shoes and Socks to People Experiencing Homeless

In my previous two service projects like this, I noticed how many people had no shoes at all.

I could only imagine how physically painful that had to be, so I knew I wanted to do a service project to address this need.

Using a gift card donation from a local store, I purchased a number of new shoes and socks in various sizes and colors.

I wanted to ensure I had enough options for people because I had no clue what anyone's size was. I could only do my best to estimate what sizes were going to be most common and proceeded with planning.

The second challenge was coming up with a way to organize the shoes so I could hand them out efficiently. Unlike the meal bags or care packages, I would need to ask someone their size and be able to quickly give them a bag with the right shoes.

I decided to label each bag and pack them into my car by size groups. Once again, I drove to downtown Dallas and started handing out shoes. My organization system did not last long, and things became a little chaotic. Everyone was so excited to get brand new shoes and socks that it created a crowd. Thankfully, I had my friend Jarrett there who did his best to help.

We ran out of shoes fast, and I was relieved that my guess-stimation of sizes was accurate. Thankfully, it was rare that I had to turn someone away because I didn't have their size.

If you want to do a project like this, you may want to consider donating items directly to a shelter or a similar organization. They may have better means to get shoes in the right hands.

If you want to do the project the way I did it, I will emphasize that you should bring someone with you. I also recommend you package the shoes into labeled crates. This should help the process go much smoother for you than it did for me.

Project #27: Hosting a Lunch for Firefighters

Another group I wanted to make sure to show appreciation for was first responders. My uncle spent many years as a firefighter, and I know that the job is especially difficult. For my twenty-seventh project, I decided to bring lunch to a local fire station.

I started this project by researching fire departments in my area and finding the best contacts to coordinate with. In my case, this was a Community Education Coordinator at my local fire department, but that may not be the case for you. Once I got in touch, we were able to set a date and time, and I was ready to start planning.

The important part was securing the food, so I started calling restaurants and caterers to find someone who could support the project. I wanted to provide a meal that was hearty but could be eaten on the go. I was able to secure the entire lunch from a Freebirds World Burrito restaurant, which I delivered to the fire station. This project went off without a hitch, and everyone appreciated the lunch.

Firefighters and first responders, in general, embody the spirit of service that I was trying to develop. Every single day, they unhesitatingly serve their communities, sometimes even putting their lives on the line for us. I encourage you to show appreciation to first responders in your community, too.

Project #28: Donating Dorm Kits to First-Generation College Students

For my twenty-eighth project, I donated kits with dorm and school essentials to low-income college students that were starting college in the fall.

When I came up with the idea for this project, I remembered how stressful dorm shopping could be. But then, I imagined how much worse it can feel for students from low-income families. Not only do they have to worry about what items they should get, but they also had the added stress of not being sure they would have the money to purchase what they needed. I wanted to help alleviate some of that stress for students.

I collaborated with a college prep organization to help a few of their students who would be starting college in the fall. I then started making a list of which items would be most helpful to incoming freshmen. This list included bedding, towels, plates and utensils, toiletries, notebooks, pens, and more.

These items may have been mundane, but they were also essentials every college student needed, so I hoped it would be a big help.

Although it would be costly to provide items for every one of the students, one of our partners stepped up to the plate. Alkami Technology allowed me to host a donation drive so that their employees could contribute items or gift cards for this project.

When I arrived at Alkami to collect the donations, I collected two bins full of items. After I put the bins in my car, I was then told to "wait a second" because their lobby was piled high with items that couldn't fit into the containers. I could not believe that so many people had donated, but thanks to everyone's generosity, I had almost everything I needed to give to the students.

Seeing all the supplies, I started planning how the service project would unfold. I originally planned to give students bins with the items already in them. However, one of the fun parts of getting ready for your first dorm is picking out items that make it your home.

I couldn't take these students to the store, but I could create our own version of a store in the event room. So, we lined up tables to create aisles that students could move between to select items. This way, each student could go on their own shopping spree.

Fast forward to the day of the service project, everything was set up and ready to go. The students came in and as soon as I told them what was going to happen, they were speechless. I don't think anyone had any idea what to say, and a few of the students didn't even believe that I was being serious.

But I was serious, and not long after, every student had a bin filled to the brim with almost everything they'd need to move in and start their first semester.

The gratitude I saw on every student's face was incredibly moving to me. Some even shed a few tears because they could not believe what was happening. Many of them told me that they had no idea how they were going to pay for the items they needed. Many of them had already started making calculations about what textbooks they may have to forego to purchase these essentials.

In that moment, I was elated to know that in some small way, I had helped these students start their college careers on a better footing, and hopefully empowered them to succeed.

QUICK TIP

If you want to support low-income and first-generation college students, you can google organizations that work with these groups and ask how you can help. Some of them already have programs that give school supplies to their students, so you may have the opportunity to volunteer with them or donate helpful items.

Project #29: Cleaning Up a Local Cemetery

For my twenty-ninth project, I decided to spend some time cleaning up an often-neglected area of communities, the cemetery. Unfortunately, many cemeteries are littered with trash and graffiti, so I wanted to help how I could.

I identified a cemetery I wanted to clean up. The day of the project, I bought a trash picker and trash bags from a local hardware store and got to work. I spent about an hour in the cemetery collecting garbage and hauling it off to a dumpster.

When my work was complete, I placed fresh flowers I had purchased. This seemed like the appropriate way to beautify this sacred space.

This was a simple project and one that I would encourage you to consider doing. You don't have to clean up cemeteries specifically. You can pick any place in your community that could use some beautifying.

You may not be the person who put the trash there, but it is nonetheless our community and our responsibility to keep it clean. Don't forget to bring a friend along - you can cover more ground and make it a more fun experience for yourself.

Project #30: Thanking My Mentor

Last but not least, I knew I had to end my 30 Days of Service journey by thanking the person who was the reason I started it in the first place, and without whom I would have never been able to complete it: my mentor, Greg Weatherford II.

I already told you about him in the last chapter, but I must emphasize how integral he was to this entire endeavor. Greg provided guidance throughout the project, and he was there for every step. If there was an obstacle I encountered, he was there to help.

So naturally, it only felt right to use my last service project to show him my appreciation. I planned an entire day for him, making sure to get him food from his favorite restaurant and plan activities like tennis, golf, and the movies.

Greg was very grateful for the day, but said he said he was prouder of me for accomplishing the journey I set out to do.

And just like that, 30 Days of Service was over.

Now What?

From July 1st to July 30th, 2019, I completed 30 different service projects that collectively impacted over 1,800 people in my community.

In total, that amounted to roughly 85 hours of direct service, not including countless hours I spent planning, contacting sponsors, gathering supplies, coordinating with nonprofits, and more.

I have to be honest, there were points where I was kicking myself wondering what possessed me to accept this arduous challenge. But those thoughts were short-lived. I will always cherish the insights I learned, some of which I'll be sharing with you in Chapter 5.

Although the 30 Days of Service initiative was complete, there were quite a few things still left to do. First though, I decided to treat myself to some sleep - a lot of it. On July 30th, I remember laying down in my bed thinking I was going to take a brief nap. Before I knew it, I was knocked out and slept for about twelve hours straight.

The next day, I got back to work so I could complete a few remaining items. One item was producing an impact report on everything I had done that I could share with the sponsors that had supported us along the way.

QUICK TIP

You should always document your work. Being able to effectively communicate your work to others is important. I encourage you to have one place where you store any projects you complete so you can share your work later with prospective employers or supporters. It's also a great way to see the growth you've made.

However, it wasn't long before I heard a familiar little voice in the back of my head. The same one that originally led to a change in my mindset and compelled me to start this service journey. Now, it was asking a new question: "What's next?"

Honestly, I was not prepared to answer that question. Having just gone through this tough journey, I was looking forward to enjoy my accomplishment. But whatever triumph I felt was drowned out by that question: "What's next?"

What *was* next?

There was no question that I was going to continue serving my community. I immensely enjoyed my experience, and I was already looking forward to another opportunity to have an impact. However, I wasn't sure what that would look like just yet. I knew that I could not keep serving at the pace I was. That would be unsustainable.

My next idea was to plan a few service projects throughout the year, which seemed like a more realistic idea. But I soon asked myself, "Could I be doing more?"

This question reminded me of how I undervalued my service in high school because it never felt impactful enough. I used to let this question discourage me from serving, but 30 Days of Service had shown me there was no reason to react that way. For one, it taught me that even the smallest acts of service make a difference. Second, if I could complete 30 service projects in 30 days, maybe I did have the ability to do more.

After some thinking, I had an answer for what was next. I decided that I was going to start my own nonprofit.

Chapter 3 Reflection Questions
After reading Chapter 3, carefully reflect on and provide responses to the following questions.

What was your favorite service project from 30 Days of Service?

Of the 30 projects, what is one that you would like to do in your community?

After reading about the service projects I completed, what community causes interested you the most?

Practicing self-care was critical to making it through 30 Days of Service. What are your self-care routines or tips that help you stay healthy, refreshed, and balanced?

What are some practical pieces of advice you can take away from my experiences planning and executing the 30 service projects?

Chapter 4
An Unexpected Chapter

Determined to Make a Difference

When I was first starting 30 Days of Service, did I have any idea I would want to start a nonprofit at the end of that? No. Did I think I knew everything about starting a nonprofit? Also no. But fresh off that experience, I felt confident that I wouldn't let what I didn't know stop me from helping others. It was time to start learning!

Thankfully, there were a million guides to refer to for starting a nonprofit, and I had one very experienced mentor to lean on. In case you're curious, here's what it takes to start a nonprofit in Texas.

First, you need Articles of Incorporation. The primary purpose of these documents is to state where and when the nonprofit was formed, along with the nonprofit's mission, membership structure, and other details.

Generally, this is pretty boilerplate, so you should be able to find templates online.

Second, you need to gather a roster of people that share your vision and/or have experience in the nonprofit area you wish to operate in.

This needs to include an incorporator, a board of directors, and a registered agent. The incorporator is who signs the articles of incorporation. This is more or less the "founder," which can be you. The board of directors is a minimum of three people (one of whom can be you) who are responsible for governing the nonprofit. Lastly, the registered agent is the person who will receive all of the legal documents for your nonprofit. The registered agent can be you, someone else, or an organization specializing in these legal documents.

Now, it's time to file this information with the Texas Secretary of State. You can do this in-person, online, or by mail. There's a $25 fee for filing this information.

You also need to register on the federal level. The first step is to get your nonprofit's employer identification number (EIN), which among other things, is needed to open a bank account. This step can be done online using an Internal Revenue Service (IRS) Form SS-4.

With this document in hand, you can apply for your 501(c)(3) status, which is what makes your nonprofit federally tax-exempt. This is done by filling out Form 1023 or 1023-EZ.

These forms are essentially the same, but you use the 1023-EZ if your nonprofit is "smaller" (i.e., it takes in less than $50,000 a year and has less than $250,000 in assets).

This final step will take anywhere between several weeks and a few months, but once you hear back from the IRS, you've done it. You have officially started a nonprofit!

Although it took some learning on my part, this process was much easier than I ever expected it to be.

FRIENDLY REMINDER

Not knowing how to do something is only ever a temporary problem. When I started 30 Days of Service and my nonprofit, I basically knew nothing. I could have let that stop me, but instead I decided to put my head down and learn. That's something I encourage you to do, too! If you don't know the first thing about what it takes to complete a project or task, then try learning about it. A lack of knowledge should never be seen as a barrier that stops your ideas. Instead, treat it as an opportunity to learn *and* accomplish something at the same time!

Oh yeah, I almost forgot to mention that you'll of course need a name. For me, deciding the name was a process that was related to the goals of the nonprofit. I knew I wanted to start the nonprofit to continue serving my community, but I also knew I wanted to do more than organize service projects.

I believed that my next step should be to create initiatives that would contribute to systemic community change and impact. The question was how did I want to do that?

After much thinking, I decided that this new nonprofit would primarily be driven by one goal: empowering young people to achieve their personal and professional potentials.

I wanted to take what I learned and pass it on to the next generation of educators, innovators, community leaders, and changemakers. I felt inspired to pursue this mission because of the experience I had teaching the life skills class in project #18. It made me want to invest in the development of youth, especially from underserved backgrounds.

With this purpose clearly defined, the name for my nonprofit became obvious: Young Leaders for Change.

Now I had a vision and a name. Then, I officially registered the organization using the steps outlined above. At this point, I felt ready to change the world.

QUICK TIP

Coming up with the perfect name for an idea can be a daunting task. Although having a good name is important, don't let that stop you from making forward progress. If all else fails, choose a straightforward name that describes your mission, like 30 Days of Service.

Taking Care of Unfinished Business

Although I was super excited for Young Leaders for Change's future, I still had some unfinished business. It was time to go back to Cornell and finish my final semester.

It was so hard to believe that three and a half years had gone by that quickly. I tried to enjoy every moment I had left while simultaneously planning for the future of my nonprofit.

The plan for 2020 consisted of a few key initiatives. The first was to host leadership classes in partnership with schools across Dallas-Fort Worth. Much like the soft skills class, this initiative's purpose was to educate youth about topics they don't normally have the opportunity to learn about, such as service-learning and entrepreneurism.

The second was to host free workshops with guest speakers, such as executives, community leaders, and athletes. Each workshop would focus on a specific skill area, with the goal of every student learning foundational skills they could apply in their daily lives. And finally, the third initiative was to continue doing service projects.

With this plan in mind, I once again started the process of finding companies to support these initiatives. Over the next several months, I put in the work to secure partnerships with organizations that could help us deliver our programming.

Fast forward to December 2019: I officially graduated from Cornell, made the long drive home, and got settled into my new life. I was excited to finally finish my college career and get back to serving!

By the time I returned home in January 2020, everything was lined up. We were set to launch our new programming in April 2020. It seemed like everything was in place and this spring was shaping up to be one of my best yet.

The Unexpected Happened

Of course, by now you know that spring 2020 brought on the global COVID-19 pandemic. Everything came to a grinding halt.

Many things that we previously took for granted before the pandemic were gone. Tragically, many peoples' lives were changed forever. At the time of writing this book, we are still amid COVID-19. My thoughts are with everyone across the world impacted by the pandemic. I am confident that we will get through this together, and we will be able to return to some sense of normalcy soon.

On a more local note, these events changed our plans for 2020. Our programming was designed to be in-person, so we had to cancel everything.

We did a lot of scrambling because we had to work with sponsors to develop alternative solutions for what we promised, but we made sure to keep a positive perspective.

We stayed positive by reminding ourselves that these were just programs, and they could be rescheduled. People were facing real crises such as being evicted from their homes, losing their jobs, and not knowing where their next meal was coming from. There was a lot of need and hurt everywhere, so our priority was to be an asset to others and help how we could.

So, we started to think - how could we help now?

QUICK TIP

As COVID-19 taught many of us, it is extremely helpful to be prepared with contingency plans. Few of us could have predicted something on the scale of a pandemic, but the takeaway is that you should try to be prepared. You should also practice being adaptable, and one way you can do this is by remembering your purpose. If you need to change plans, remember your purpose, and make adjustments that allow you to still accomplish it.

Our Collective New Normal

One of the first things that we came to realize at the start of the pandemic was how little was known about it.

Even worse, there seemed to be conflicting information. Not only about the pandemic itself, but also how we should be personally getting our lives back on track and how we should adjust to this new normal. It was like everyone was fumbling around in the dark, especially people from my generation.

This was the first major crisis of my generation, and we faced unprecedented challenges ahead. For example, how were we supposed to navigate online schooling at an age where social interactions are crucial for mental health? How were young professionals supposed to find jobs during this time?

People of all ages faced questions like these, but this was especially true for people my age. The uniqueness of the situation and how it was evolving rapidly created heightened confusion.

Thriving Together

To tackle this problem, we launched our first pandemic-focused initiative in April 2020, called "Let's Thrive Now." This was a free website that served as a go-to hub for young people to get all the information they would need to navigate the challenges of the pandemic.

The website provided resources on a range of topics such as financial literacy, mental health, career development, and physical wellness. This project meant we had to compile a wide variety of articles and create videos featuring experts.

Our primary goal was to help young people make it through the pandemic. However, we also wanted them to know that it was still possible to grow and achieve their goals during this time. For example, we advocated using this time to connect with more people virtually, since everyone suddenly found themselves with more free time.

Now I know you're probably thinking: so, all you did was collect articles and put them in one spot?

Yes. But like I said, this site filled a critical need for many young people: a trusted place they could go to get all the advice they could need to thrive during the pandemic. And the response we received was overwhelming. Since we launched the site, we have helped thousands of young people get important information to help them succeed during this difficult time.

I spent most of summer 2020 working on Let's Thrive Now. We were regularly adding more articles to adapt to a swiftly changing crisis and interviewing more experts to provide unique insights and knowledge.

QUICK TIP

Although finding information is easier than ever because of the internet, it is difficult to find *accurate* information. Everyone has a platform to spread information, which provides the opportunity for uninformed opinions and disinformation to spread; so, how can you know what to trust? First and foremost, you need to always know your sources and think about their goals. Who owns the source you get your news from? Who's reporting on it? Did someone pay for the article or post you're reading? All of these factors should be considered. This is a complex topic, so I encourage you to independently learn more about identifying misinformation and disinformation.

Mentor Moments

Although Let's Thrive Now had helped many young people, I felt that it was time to do more. As we were approaching fall, we started thinking about how many internships had been canceled because of the pandemic.

Like many college students, my internships were critical to my professional growth and career prospects. I could only imagine the devastation young people felt by losing those opportunities.

We knew thousands of students missed out on building up their resumes, learning new skills, and most importantly, receiving mentorship during their internships. Although we could not replace those internships, we wanted to help. We felt the least we could do was offer young people a way to receive those crucial professional lessons they would have gotten if it wasn't for the pandemic.

Eventually, Greg suggested we start a podcast. His idea was this: our podcast would interview executives, who would offer advice that could be useful to young people. Our goal was to make every episode feel like the conversation you would have if you had the opportunity to sit down for coffee with the guest.

Inspired by this vision, we decided to call the show "Mentor Moments."

I instantly loved the idea, and so over the next few weeks, we went to work creating the podcast. It was a sprint. From when we conceptualized the idea to when we published our first episodes in September 2020 was only three weeks. In that timeframe, we ironed out the format for the show, built the branding, created a website, and produced the episodes.

One of the most surprising things to me was how many executives were eager to support this project. Admittedly, I went into this podcast thinking that everyone would be too busy to help. After all, they are normally saddled with work, and I imagined that the workload had only increased with the pandemic. However, many of them responded positively.

Soon, I was fortunate to have brilliant leaders appear on the show, such as Cynt Marshall, CEO of the Dallas Mavericks, Dolf Berle, CEO of Topgolf, and Arjun Dugal, CTO of Capital One Financial Services.

Like with any other service project, if you go into it with an open mind, you can learn from your service, and I learned a lot from this podcast. I encourage you to listen for yourself because there is beneficial advice in these episodes. In the interim, I'll highlight some of my favorite tips from our guests.

First, I want to highlight something that Cynt Marshall told me in Episode 8: know what you value and what you won't compromise on because that is what will let you feel good about getting up every day and going to work.

This advice resonated with me, and I think it's important for all of us. As an exercise, I encourage you to define your key principles and values. These may change over your lifetime, but being aware of these will guide your daily life decisions.

Another one of my favorite pieces of advice was shared by Stephen Bohanon, co-founder of Alkami Technology, who was featured in Episode 14.

At one point, he emphasized the importance of the people you include in your life. If you want to be successful, you must have people around you who have already been where you want to go so you can learn from them. It's also important to be around people who are as ambitious and driven as you.

This advice gave me much to think about, and I feel that it is something many young people need to hear. I've been guilty of keeping people around in my life that were not the best influences. Learning to let go of these people was a crucial lesson I learned.

Sometimes these decisions will be hard and can even make us feel lonely. However, tough decisions like these can be necessary for our growth. So, I was appreciative that he shared this insight.

FRIENDLY REMINDER

You've heard this a million times before, but it's true that you need to love yourself before loving others. This holds true for romantic relationships and friendships. When we don't love ourselves, we will make decisions that can compromise or hurt us just so we can keep other people around and not feel lonely. Moving forward, let's do better. We deserve it! We owe it to ourselves to think about what a good friend looks like and what we expect from our partners. We are worthy of friendships and relationships that are healthy, supportive, and bring out the best in us.

The last advice I want to share was from Dr. Sejal Hathi, a resident physician at Massachusetts General Hospital, who appeared in Episode 15.

When asked how young people can find great mentors and network with others, she provided some straightforward but actionable advice.

She suggested reaching out to people with clear intentions. Don't just ask someone to get coffee, ask to pick their brains on specific topics or questions.

After your meeting, follow up with the person you connected with. If they gave you advice, share an update a few months down the road to show that they had an impact on you.

Lastly, don't be afraid to give back to them, too. Offer to help however you can and share your perspectives.

I loved the simple but effective nature of this advice, and it felt especially important to share given the theme of the show.

Eighteen weeks and twenty episodes later, we concluded our very first season, and it was an amazing journey. I could not be more thankful to our guests for taking the time to invest in other young people.

A Continued Commitment

So, this is how we pivoted our plans to serve others.

Of course, 2020 looked drastically different from how I thought it would. But I'm grateful to have had the opportunity to still help others in such a turbulent year.

Frankly, serving my community became a source of solace for me. With so much going on in the world that felt out of my control, it was comforting to know I could still make a difference and inspire others.

What are our plans for the future? For many reasons, these are going to be some of the most important years of our lives as we deal with the fallout of a hotly contested election and work to get lives back to normal with the end of coronavirus in sight. There are many opportunities for us to do impactful and transformative work.

I'm excited to share more about our plans with you in the next chapter. But first, let's go over some of the insights I learned from my experiences.

Chapter 4 Reflection Questions

After reading Chapter 4, carefully reflect on and provide responses to the following questions.

How did COVID-19 affect any life plans you had? What are ways that you adapted to the challenges you faced?

What are things that COVID-19 made you realize you took for granted?

What other lessons have you taken away from the COVID-19 pandemic?

Moving forward, how do you want to challenge yourself to better handle adversity?

Chapter 5
Insights to Live By

What This Journey Taught Me

You now know the story that led me to where I am today. Though not every step of the journey was easy, all of it was important for discovering more about myself and how I could make a difference in the world.

I learned so many things over the past few years, but here are 4 insights that particularly stand out.

Insight #1: Embrace Our Differences

As I mentioned to you in Chapter 1, I grew up in a bubble. It was your typical American suburb, and we were a typical middle-class family. The only cultures and perspectives I was exposed to were those in my city, and they shaped my vision for my future.

I only started to experience the world outside of my bubble through my summer 2016 internship and my experiences at Cornell. I learned from diverse perspectives, backgrounds, cultures, and community issues that made me question how I approached life. Had I remained ignorant, it's almost certain that I would never have discovered the life trajectory I am on today. That would have been a shame because I am happier with my future than I ever have been.

My experience highlights just one reason why it is important for all of us to be comfortable with and seek out differences. There is much that we have to learn from each other, and we are only putting ourselves at a disadvantage when we remain in comfortable familiarity.

I encourage you to expose yourself to new ideas, cultures, and people that you may never have thought of interacting with. At the very least, you'll become a more knowledgeable person. At best, you will gain some revelatory knowledge that can positively impact your life, like I did.

Additionally, how we choose to embrace differences is vital to the lifeblood of our communities. Unfortunately, we have thousands of recent examples of what happens when we choose to reject, rather than accept, differences between people and ideas. We live in a more polarized society than ever before. Part of that is because not enough people have decided to learn from their neighbors who disagree with them or look different than they do. So, I encourage you to be part of the change by exploring differences, rather than becoming more insular in the face of them.

How can you seek out and learn from differences? If you are in an environment that is naturally diverse, like cities and some college campuses, then this is relatively easy for you. Choose to (safely) explore neighborhoods that you have not been to. Find new groups to hang out with. Try eating at a new restaurant serving unfamiliar cuisine. Experiences like these are easily accessible to you, so tap into them.

If your environment isn't diverse like the previous examples, then it will take some more deliberate action to seek out different perspectives. Embrace researching as a substitute for in-person experiences. You can watch documentaries that highlight different perspectives, attend festivals that promote different cultures, read about diverse history, and more.

Whatever your situation may be, I hope you will heed this advice. It's natural to surround ourselves with what is familiar to us, so make the effort to break this norm. It is how we can make progress and create better communities.

Insight #2: Live on Purpose

Over the past four years, I learned how important it is to think about the purpose of everything I do, no matter how small. Whether it is a school project, a service initiative, or a house chore, I must think about why I'm doing it.

You might be wondering, "Why?" I have learned that whether you know it or not, the purpose behind why you're doing something will influence your decisions. If you don't set a good purpose, then you probably won't produce a good outcome.

Here's an example. Let's say you need to go to the grocery store. This is an errand that annoys you, so your mindset towards it automatically becomes negative, and you rush to complete the task.

Because you're trying to finish your errand quickly, you might not bother making a list since that'd take additional time. You're probably not going to price shop carefully, because you're trying to grab everything and get out. By the time you get home, you might end up realizing you didn't get some items that you needed (necessitating another grocery trip) and spent more than you needed to (costing you money).

Now let's try again, but this time, you take a moment to think about your purpose. You don't like going to the grocery store, but you recognize it's an essential task, so you will ensure this one trip will get you everything you need.

Because you know that's your purpose, you'll probably decide it's helpful to see what's already in your kitchen. Then you'll probably decide to make a list so you don't forget anything. At the store, you'll decide to check everything against your list. When you get home, you have everything you need, and you won't have to go to the store for at least a week.

Does the second approach take more time? In the moment, yes. In the long term, no.

You saved yourself time because you were deliberate about making sure you did the task as effectively as possible. By defining a better purpose before rushing into "do it" mode, you had a better outcome.

I know that's a simple example, but it illustrates my point. You should take this sort of approach with everything you do.

Eventually, it will become a habit. Trust me, you will quickly notice a difference. You will be happier with the work you do, you will use your time more efficiently, and you will be more effective all-around. It is worth your time to live on purpose.

> **QUICK TIP**
> It's helpful to try and come up with a comprehensive list of action items for any project, task, or business. When you try to complete something without first thinking about everything that needs to be done, you can add more stress to the situation. After defining the purpose or goal for a project, sit down and think critically about every step you will need to take and try to put a deadline to it. This list will help you accomplish your purpose.

Insight #3: Think Like an Entrepreneur

I grew up watching a lot of Shark Tank. I loved hearing the outlandish ideas, the sharks' commentary, and the drama.

But honestly, I never learned much from watching the show.

That's not a knock on the producers, it's my fault. Although I thought the show was fun to watch, I never thought that it would be relevant to my life because I was going to focus on building up a career at a company.

Now that I do consider myself an entrepreneur, I wish I had paid more attention to the show. But whether you're going to be an entrepreneur or not, there is a lot we can learn from the entrepreneurial mindset.

Let me tell you why. Being "entrepreneurial" is about more than starting your own company. It's a set of skills that will help you in everything you'll do in life. Most importantly, this means being self-reliant and taking initiative.

I'll break these two concepts down.

When you don't know something, or feel like you've hit a wall on a task, what do you do? Do you give up? Do you ask for help? Sometimes those are the appropriate responses, but thinking like an entrepreneur means that the first thing you do is try to figure it out.

That is what being self-reliant means. This is an important character trait because it equips you to overcome challenges you may face in life.

You will only grow this trait through practice. Whenever you encounter a tough problem, make an effort to solve it on your own. Work through it with logic or research it to understand how to overcome it. You may not always be successful, but at the very least, you will learn and become more self-reliant.

When you do figure out a problem through hard work, it will grow your confidence. For example, when I started 30 Days of Service, I didn't know if I could do it. I had no idea how to plan it. Yet, I told myself I'd figure it out. As I worked through more issues, made decisions, and executed projects, I proved to myself I could accomplish complex tasks and carried that confidence into the rest of my work.

Being self-reliant may take more time than asking for help, but it is often worth it for the learning and confidence you can gain from it.

The other part of thinking like an entrepreneur is taking initiative. That can mean a lot of things, but to me, it means meeting opportunity wherever it is.

This is important because one of the biggest differences between successful people and everyone else is that they tend to take initiative. There have been many brilliant ideas that went on Shark Tank, but there have also been plenty of not-so-good ideas that still managed to find success.

The key is not necessarily the idea itself. It's the fact that these people put themselves out there and took action.

In your case, taking the initiative could mean volunteering to accept an extra credit project. It could also mean proposing a solution to a problem you noticed at work. Basically, if you see an opportunity to do something that can create value, take a shot at it.

Having initiative is what can help you grow more, stand out from others, and bring you success. Now, I'm not telling you to chase every idea that comes to mind. But never let a lack of initiative stand between you and success.

These are not the only skills that entrepreneurs use to be successful, but these are skills that I've learned will always serve you well.

QUICK TIP

If you want to evaluate whether an idea is good or not, you can use a S.W.O.T. Analysis (created by Albert Humphrey). It's simple to use. For any idea, business, or project you have, identify its strengths and weaknesses, then external opportunities and threats that can affect it. Thinking about your ideas in this way will help you logically determine whether it is something you should explore further. To learn more about this process, Google the term S.W.O.T. Analysis for examples and case studies.

Insight #4: Never Be Afraid to Ask for Help

I know this sounds contradictory to what I said about self-reliance, but I promise, it's not.

Part of being self-reliant is knowing your limits and when you should ask for help. Sometimes there's no replacement for the experience and wisdom of people that have done it before.

Never be afraid to ask for help. It's not a sign of weakness. People have rarely accomplished great things without even a little bit of help. That being said, when you do need to ask for help, it's important to know exactly what kind of help you need.

When you're starting a project, ask yourself: what are your weaknesses? What are your knowledge gaps? What skills do you lack? Knowing these answers will enable you to seek out the right kind of help.

Additionally, don't be afraid to ask somebody for help because of their job title. Sometimes you'll get a yes, sometimes you'll get a no. But that's the worst that can happen, so ask.

You've probably heard that phrase a million times before, so let me give you another reason you should ask.

Oftentimes, successful people are happy to help you because they once had to ask others for help. Most see helping others, especially young people, as a way to give back. So, if you've done your homework, identified exactly what you need help with, and have asked politely, you will be surprised by how many people will be happy to assist you.

One last thing - don't forget to practice gratitude. It's never a guarantee that people will help you. When someone does take the time to help you, please make sure you let them know that you appreciate it.

At a minimum, make sure to send a thank you email. But if you want to go the extra mile, send a handwritten thank you card. It may seem like an inconvenience, but the extra effort you put into it is not going to be lost on the person receiving it.

Let's Be Better Together

So, now you're caught up on my story. It's been quite a ride for me, and I hope that it's inspired you in some way.

I don't know your specific situation, your goals, or what your plans are for the future. But I do know that you are more than capable of accomplishing great things. Don't settle for less than what you want out of life.

If you don't know what that is yet, that is okay. That is the fun part of life: learning, growing, and figuring it out. Your life won't always be perfect - nothing ever is. But if you embrace the journey and hard work, it will be a positive experience.

But before you go, I do want to ask you one favor.

There are many challenges that we are facing. Of course, this includes a significant amount of healing after a tumultuous four years and a contentious election. It includes getting through what is hopefully the last phase of the pandemic and getting everyone back up on their feet. But it also includes issues that have plagued us for some time now, such as hunger, homelessness, access to education, racism, inequity, disinformation, climate change, and so much more.

No single person can tackle these issues alone. If we want to see a better world for ourselves and future generations, then we must stand united and embrace truth, service, education, diversity, equity, science, kindness, and empathy. We must work tirelessly to advocate and advance these values.

We must embrace the differences we have with each other, love those who don't look like us, stand up for those who have been systematically oppressed, and work together until we are all treated equally.

We recognize now that fostering togetherness is the key to bettering our communities and creating a better future. With that in mind, we have adopted a new name for our nonprofit: the Better Together Foundation.

I ask that you join me in this commitment by taking the Better Together pledge. This is a commitment to be a role model and make a difference in whatever way you can.

The Pledge
I, _____, pledge to do the following:

1. Support and be kind to all living beings regardless of race, gender, socio-economic status, or any other qualities that may make them different from me;
2. Embrace learning more about the world around me, especially other cultures and viewpoints that I may not be familiar with or understand;
3. Advocate for the rights of and respect for people who may normally be marginalized in communities or conversations in school, the workplace, social media, and anywhere else, and
4. Make time to serve my community, however I can, whether that is saying thank you to people who show me kindness, volunteering at a soup kitchen, or doing something else.

I'm sure by now you're asking, "what's next for you?" I'm going to continue finding ways to give back to the community. Specifically, the Better Together Foundation will continue to work towards our mission. We will provide enrichment to the lives of youth across the country in the areas of service-learning, entrepreneurism, physical and mental wellness, lifelong learning, and professionalism.

How do we plan to accomplish that? There are many ways we can help close racial and economic opportunity gaps for youth, especially minority youth.

Right now, we're exploring ideas like launching a mobile app that can help kids find mentors, opening a youth center to create a safe space to learn and play, an incubator, and opening a media studio that provides youth with an outlet to create positive content for the masses.

Although I don't know exactly what the future looks like yet, I'm eager to join you in changing the world. Let's go have an impact because if there's one thing I know, it's that we're **BETTER TOGETHER**.

Chapter 5 Reflection Questions

After reading Chapter 5, carefully reflect on and provide responses to the following questions.

How can you become more inclusive and supportive of people that are different from you?

In what ways do you think like an entrepreneur? What are ways you can think more entrepreneurially?

What kind of help could you benefit from right now?

Who are the types of mentors you should seek to help you reach your goals?

Which of these insights resonated with you most? How can you apply this insight to your daily life?

If you had to write a two - three sentence purpose statement that guides your life, what would it be?

What are some ways you want to impact the world? Think about both small and big ways you can have an impact - both are equally important.

Practical Tips

I want to share some of the tips and methods I've used for approaching different tasks. These are by no means the definitive ways to accomplish anything I discuss here; this is just what has worked for me. I encourage you to find what works best for you.

Setting Goals

Setting goals is an important step to living on purpose. So, let me share with you some best practices for setting effective goals.

It's simple. In fact, if you've ever thought about a New Year's resolution, you've already done this before. I start the goal-setting process by thinking about outcomes that I want to happen. This could mean getting a 3.5 GPA in the next college semester, saving a certain amount of money this year, and more.

These outcomes are what I'm primarily working towards, but there may be multiple goals that build up to them. For example, if you want to own a house in 10 years, you may have a goal to set aside a certain amount of money in 8 years so you can afford the down payment. To identify all of these goals, work backwards from your ultimate desired outcome.

This is how I set goals, and it's a process I repeat often. I recommend you do this *at least* once a month because your goals can often change. Readjust your plans as needed to make sure that you are always on the right track and making progress.

Eventually, once you build up the habit, you'll want to set goals for every week and even every day.

Balancing a Heavy Workload

In life, there are going to be times when you feel like you have a lot going on and it's hard to juggle it all. That's totally normal, but there are plenty of ways you can cope with that feeling and manage a heavy workload.

If you're ever feeling overwhelmed, don't immediately give up. I encourage you to try and make it all work. Sometimes, you have taken on too much and it is necessary to drop a few things. There's no shame in that, but make sure it's the right decision for you. Be wise in what you drop: target things that can free you up or are less important to you.

In my experience, the key to balancing work is always being aware of the work and their deadlines. This is important for planning out when you will work on certain tasks. So, building a comprehensive to-do list is vital.

This is easy to do with schoolwork, especially in college. Most syllabi you get from your professors will list dates for assignments and tests. You can put all of these due dates into a blank document or to-do list.

It'll be tedious, but you only have to do it once a semester. Trust me, it is useful to be able to look at everything you're going to need to do across all your classes.

With your job or your projects, this process can be trickier. Tasks and due dates may not be clear, and they may often change. The best thing you can do is follow the goal-setting tips I discussed above to identify major items to be aware of. That will help you understand what you need to work towards, as well as a timeline for accomplishing them.

Once you have a grasp on everything you must do, you should start plotting out when you will work on certain items. Plan strategically to balance your workload. If you have five assignments due on one day, maybe you should plan to work on one or a few of them earlier than the rest, so you're not working on all five at once.

The worst thing you can do when you feel overwhelmed is to not have a firm understanding of your to-do list. Avoid this stress by making it easy for you to tackle everything that needs to get done.

Maximizing Your Day

While we're discussing the topic of productivity, let's address something very important: you should make a schedule for yourself every day! Making a schedule allows you to be deliberate about how you spend your time. It makes going through each day easy because it saves you from the effort of coming up with plans on the spot.

So, let me tell you how I make a schedule.

I start by making a list of everything I need to fit into my day. For me, this includes breakfast, lunch, and dinner, a nap, meetings, work time, family time, and time for myself (which can include hanging out with friends, working out, etc.). Then, I decide how many hours to allot to these components.

Now, I'm able to make my schedule. I first put in everything firm, such as my meetings. I plan the rest of my schedule components around those. Personally, I prioritize fitting in work, followed by family time, a nap, meals, then time for me. This approach allows me to accomplish everything I want to in a day.

Try it out for yourself and see the difference - you might be surprised how much you enjoy living by a schedule.

Planning Projects and Events

Throughout this book, you may have been wondering how you would even begin to plan a project or event on your own. Based on my experience planning many of these over the past five years, unfortunately, I don't know of any simple formula. Each project and event can be very different from the other. That being said, there are still some common steps you can follow.

Like most things, it starts with purpose. I always think about my intended outcomes for a project or event so I know how to make my planning decisions.

Next, I make sure to identify my audience. Whom am I serving with this project, or who will be coming to this event? This is as important as the purpose because you need to make sure everything is appropriate for your audience.

With these details in mind, I start building out the idea. There are questions that I tend to always ask myself. What is going to happen? If it's an event, what are the different phases of it? If it's a service project, what exactly will I do to help people? Answering these questions will help you flesh out your idea and give you all the pieces you need to plan for.

Let's pretend you're planning a breakfast at a senior center. The major components you'll have to consider include what kind of food will be served? How will it be served? How will you set up? What are you going to be doing during the breakfast? What all will you have to clean up after?

Outline specific steps for these components. Personally, it helps me to imagine walking through the day. This allows me to build out a rough schedule and map out steps.

For this example, I know the day will start with picking up breakfast. I don't know where I'll be getting it from yet, so that's a step: find a restaurant that will donate food.

I'll need to put the food in my car and have a way to safely carry it to the venue. So, that's another step: put a box in my car to carry the food before I go pick it up.

Next, I'll drive to the senior center and start setting up. I want to set up a buffet line, so I will need tables that can fit all of the food. I don't know for sure that the center will have tables, so another step is to bring my folding tables.

Write down all the steps that come to mind so you don't miss anything. Once you have your steps laid out, prioritize them. Think about what you can't do before moving forward to the next step. For example, you can't know how much food to order from the restaurant until you ask the senior center how many seniors you'll be serving.

With all your steps in order, start putting a timeline on your list. Work backward from the date of the project or event so you plan accordingly.

Finally, one thing I always do is put together a checklist for myself. Usually, this has a schedule of the project or event and items that I need to do at specific times. This helps ensure I stay on track and don't miss anything. It makes life easier - instead of trying to keep track of everything in my mind, I can look at my list and know what needs to happen next.

Making Budgets

Budgets are essential for making your ideas for projects, businesses, and events come to life. So how do you make a budget? Don't feel overwhelmed. Thankfully, it does not take an accounting degree to make an effective budget.

Start by thinking about all the expenses you may have to incur. It can be hard to try and brainstorm that from scratch, so I find it helpful to imagine executing each step of the project like I did in the previous tip. Once I have my steps on paper, I can start to make a list of my expenses.

Now that I have a list, I try to assign realistic costs for each expense. If the expense is a physical item, the best way to estimate prices is by researching and price shopping online.

If the expense is something more intangible or highly variable, like labor expenses, then you're going to need to do more in-depth research. Look up articles, find estimates, or get a sense of what that type of expense usually costs by looking at sites where these types of services are offered.

After you have assigned costs to each expense, it is wise to add another 10 - 20% on top of your estimate. This ensures you're accounting for any possible increases in costs or unexpected expenses. Remember, it's always better to come in under budget than over! If you end up not using the extra amount you budgeted, then you can put that back into your project.

Once your budget is finalized, I recommend reviewing it to see how you can cut down expenses. See what can possibly be covered by a donation if you're doing a charitable project.

There are many other methods to making a budget, so learn more about this topic by researching online.

Finding Sponsors and Supporters

Support comes in many different forms, most commonly through monetary donations, in-kind donations (i.e. items given to you for free), and knowledge. For now, I'm going to focus on monetary and in-kind donations.

The first step is to decide what support you need and how exactly it will be used. If you need monetary donations, then you should have a clear plan for how you'll use them.

Next, you need to identify people that might be interested in providing the support you need. It's important to consider the scope of your project when finding sponsors. Specifically, you should think about whether the project serves a need that the sponsor cares about. Most companies publicly state their community focuses. Generally, if your project does not align with one of the company's charitable focuses, they will be less likely to support it, so keep this in mind.

Considering how much support you need will also help you determine what kind of sponsor to target. If you're looking for a monetary or in-kind donation of less than $1,000, then you may want to consider companies or businesses that are locally owned.

If the support you need is more than that, then you may want to consider approaching mid-sized, large, or even national companies. It may be harder to get in touch with these kinds of businesses, but they will have the resources you need.

After I've decided these parameters, I research businesses, organizations, and other possible sponsors in my area that meet those criteria. One way I do this is by looking at local business journals. They often have lists such as the most charitable companies, fastest-growing mid-sized companies. This is a great resource to help you find prospects.

Writing Professional Emails

One of the best skills you can learn is how to write effective emails! You would be surprised how rare this skill is for many people, especially among young adults. If you can write high-quality emails, you will stand out and increase your chances of getting an interview, receiving support for your projects, obtaining extensions on papers, and more.

I start by thinking about the intended outcome of the email. Remember, no one likes reading long emails, so keep it brief.

Second, always start with a pleasantry. Don't immediately jump into your point or question. That can seem rude and self-centered. When you're starting a new email conversation with someone, your first sentence should be something like, "I hope this email finds you doing well." Starting with a salutation conveys friendliness and creates a better first impression.

Third, use your first paragraph to set up the context for your email. Again, keep it short, but let the person know why you're reaching out in the first place. By the end of the first paragraph, your recipient should at least know what the point of the discussion is.

Fourth, on the topic of paragraphs - please, please don't make them too long. People's eyes start glazing over whenever they read a long paragraph, so I make sure my paragraphs are four to six lines long (lines, not sentences). This will make your emails much easier to read.

Fifth, avoid sounding entitled or ungrateful. This is another mistake that people often make. There are a few ways to avoid this. For example, if you're making a request, make sure to include a "please." A good phrase to use is, "Would you please consider..."

It is also helpful to thank the person before they even help you. You can do this by including phrases like, "Thank you in advance for your time," or, "Thank you in advance for any insights or suggestions you may have."

Finally, always edit your email once it's written. Start by checking for the obvious, like spelling or grammar errors. Then, look for ways you can make it more concise or clear.

If you follow these tips, you will write more effective emails and receive better responses.

Finding Mentors

Finding a mentor is something that can be life changing. They can be an indispensable resource to teach you lessons, encourage you, and much more. Here's my advice on how I would find and connect with mentors.

First of all, it's useful to think about what kind of mentor would be helpful to you.

Although mentors come in many forms, it's easiest to start by finding someone who is in a spot in life you want to eventually reach. These are people who will likely have the experience you want to learn from.

Don't limit yourself - think big! For example, if you want to work in technology, reach out to Vice Presidents of Technology or even Chief Technology Officers. It never hurts to send an email (as long as you do it politely), and you never know who will be willing to talk to you.

Now that you know what types of people to reach out to, start identifying specific ones. If you're interested in connecting with executives and other high-level leaders, that information can usually be found on a company's website. However, if you're looking for people at the manager level or below, they can be harder to locate.

Linkedin is a good tool to use. If you search for any company, click on their company page, and then click on "People." You will see a list of people associated with the company. You can scroll through everyone, or you can refine your search even more. This will help you find the best person to connect with.

After finding who you want to speak to, it's time to send your message. You can do this through Linkedin, or you can send an email if you have it. You could just ask them to chat or get coffee sometime, but that's not the most effective approach. That is vague and doesn't give the person much of a reason to respond.

Instead, be specific with why you would like to speak to the person. That will help you get responses because not only does it let the person know whether or not they will be able to give you the advice you're looking for, it also shows you're serious and will benefit from their time.

Let's say you're reaching out to the executive director of a nonprofit. An example of a good message to send is, "I'm interested in learning more about serving my community. I was wondering if we could have a quick chat so I could learn how you plan and organize service projects?"

The last piece of advice I'll mention is that you should show you're being considerate of the person's time. They are likely busy, so don't ask for an hour-long chat. A good place to start is by politely asking the person for 15 - 30 minutes of their time.

Maximizing Mentorship

Now, you may be wondering how you can make the most of a mentor's time. The key is to be thoughtful and have a plan.

Before going into any chat with a mentor, you should always have questions and topics in mind. It is good to outline a rough agenda.

However, treat your agenda as a useful guide, not a script. You should strive to have a conversation, not a Q&A interview. Use these questions to start a conversation about different topics you want to know about, but ask follow-up questions, too. Don't just robotically move from topic-to-topic.

After your meeting, grow your relationship with the mentor by making sure to say thank you. You can also follow up with them to share specific ways their advice impacted you. Moving forward, ask this person to catch up once periodically.

Lastly, to maximize your mentorship, make it clear that you're happy to help your mentor in any way you can. I know that may sound backwards since you're the one being mentored. However, it's a good way to show that you are considerate and want to invest in them, too.

Finding Email Addresses

Finding emails is a useful skill that can let you get in touch with prospective mentors, ask companies to support your projects, send a note to a hiring manager, and more. However, email addresses tend to be difficult to find. Thankfully, there are tools that can help.

Two tools have been helpful to me: a website called hunter.io, and a Chrome plugin called Clearbit Connect. Disclaimer: I'm by no means an expert in how these services work, so the explanations I'll provide are based on my experiences using them.

To utilize these tools, you simply have to type in the domain (e.g. allbettertogether.org) for the organization you're wanting to connect with. Then, they will attempt to find every email associated with the domain. They aren't always effective, but at the very least, they can show you how a company formats its emails.

Usually, companies use similar formats for every employee's email. So, if you know the format for one person, you can guess what another person's email is.

If you have no luck at all, then there are a few common formats companies tend to use for emails. With trial-and-error, you may be able to find the right email address.

Here are some of the most common email address formats - you usually will be able to get one of these to work.

1. firstname@company.com
2. firstnamelastname@company.com
3. firstname.lastname@company.com
4. firstinitiallastname@company.com
5. firstnamelastinitial@company.com

Presenting My Ideas

There will be times where you need to present your ideas to someone to receive their support. To maximize these opportunities, you need to build a pitch that can get people behind your idea.

First, you need to be able to summarize your idea. Your pitch will go nowhere if people don't understand what you're talking about. You should start by making sure you can condense your idea into one or two sentences. In general, the summary of your idea should look like "We should do *these things* to create *these outcomes*," or "This business offers *these services* to *these customers*."

After defining your idea, elaborate on it. What exactly you should communicate in your presentation depends on your audience and the purpose of the meeting. This isn't always an easy determination to make, so consider what your audience is most interested in hearing. For example, if you're seeking to gain support for a smaller scale service project, you may not want to spend a lot of time talking about your budget.

Here are some talking points you can include in almost any pitch:

- The Problem
- Your Idea (i.e. the summary above)
- Business Model/How It'll Happen
- Customers/People Served
- Expected Outcomes

It's also prudent to create a list of questions you think you'll be asked. It can be tricky to come up with questions, but try to imagine that you're hearing your pitch for the first time. What questions would you have? You can also give your pitch to a friend, mentor, or someone else you trust and see what they ask you.

Something to keep in mind is that people will naturally be skeptical of you if you're young. This isn't always true, but some people will think you are either a know-it-all or out of your depth just because of your age.

Don't let that deter or discourage you. There are ways to overcome this mentality.

One is to address this skepticism by "disarming" doubts before your audience even raises them. For example, if you expect to be asked what your plan is for building a new business, give an overview of that in your presentation. You can mention challenges you expect to encounter. Addressing questions before they're asked demonstrates that you have thought ahead and are not being naive.

Another strategy is to establish your credibility. You can show results from previous projects you have done (like data, testimonials, articles, etc.). This may not be an option for you yet. If that's the case, there are still a couple of things you can do.

For example, you can share how previous experiences have given you skills or knowledge related to your pitch. You can explain how you've studied something relevant to the pitch in class, or how you learned about it on your own.

You can also mention how you've spoken about your idea with mentors. This helps the audience know the idea has been vetted by other people.

However, don't try too hard to establish your credibility, especially if you don't think you can make a convincing case. You run the risk of seeming like you're insecure, increasing the audience's skepticism.

Regardless of how you choose to establish credibility in your presentation, the most important piece of advice I have is do not ever lie. Not only is it wrong to do, but it will rarely work and is likely to backfire on you horribly.

Don't try to make up for a shaky idea or a lack of credibility by lying - it will never work.

Leading Meetings

Meetings are oftentimes the only chance you have to make an impression on someone, so you should do everything you can to get it right.

Start by thinking about why you want to have a meeting. Is a meeting the best way to accomplish that purpose, or can it be easily discussed through an email or Slack message? Is it necessary for everyone you are planning to invite to be there?

Asking yourself these questions is important because people are wary of meetings. In the workplace, people generally see them as inefficient time sinks. That's because they may be used to attending ineffective meetings, but your meetings will not fall into that category.

Now that you have identified your purpose and decided that a meeting is necessary, you need to plan an agenda. This should be a list of the major topics you want to discuss, and possibly a list of questions.

Here's an example of what your agenda might look like.

- Introductions
- Meeting Purpose
    - Discussion
    - Question 1
    - Question 2
    - Question 3
- Next Steps

If you're responsible for sending out a calendar invite for a meeting, it should contain all of the pertinent information. In addition to your agenda, you should include the context for the meeting, the location (or Zoom link), the list of attendees, and anything else that could be a useful reference for the meeting attendees.

Once in the meeting, I recommend starting the conversation by succinctly restating the desired outcome of the meeting. This ensures everyone is on the same page.

Be sure to pay close attention to the time, because you should try to ensure your meetings do not run over. If you're the main person talking in the meeting, then pace yourself and leave enough time for discussion and questions. If you're guiding the conversation, try to keep the conversation focused. Don't be afraid to gently start wrapping up the meeting 5 minutes before the official end time.

Finally, conclude every meeting with a recap of next steps. This ensures everyone leaves with the same understanding.

Building a Professional Reputation

My mentor once told me that the most valuable currency you have is your professional reputation. The reputation you have is like money. You must work hard to get it, you have access to more opportunities if you have it, and if you aren't careful, you can lose it. So, how can you build up your reputation?

You must deliver quality work. There's no shortcut or helpful tip to get around this part. This is the basis of your reputation. What "quality work" looks like depends on what the task is in the first place. At the very least, this means ensuring your work never looks sloppy. After you finish a task, be sure to check for grammar or spelling errors, wrong information, inconsistencies, and other errors that can make it seem like you cut corners.

Generally, it's a good idea to under-promise but over-deliver. When you accept a task, don't make lofty promises. Just go above and beyond in what you produce. If you can set the deadline, you should consider requesting more time than you need so you can deliver the task early.

By following these steps, you will build a reputation for delivering work that is more than expected and always ahead of schedule.

You should also strive to make it unnecessary for people to ask for an update. You will make a strong impression if you are so dependable that nobody needs to wonder about the status of a task. If appropriate, send updates to your manager as you complete steps in a task or project.

Lastly, the most important component of your professional reputation is being honest. Ways to demonstrate honesty include being accountable for your mistakes, never seeming like you are taking credit for others' work, and never going behind someone's back.

You should also make a habit of speaking your mind if you have a well-informed opinion. However, you should be aware that there is a fine line between being straightforward and being rude. It is good to share your thoughts, but make sure that you are always polite, respectful, and thoughtful when you do so.

Creating Impressive Documents and Presentations

Delivering presentations and documents that are appealing and convey information well can make a strong impression. How you do this depends on the purpose of the deliverable, the audience, the context of delivery, and more, but below are some general rules that can help you.

For one, you should start by thinking about the structure of your presentation or document. Like a well-written essay, the order you present information to the reader is important. It needs to flow in a way that tells a story.

To illustrate what I mean, you wouldn't want to tell someone how to solve a problem if you haven't even told them about the problem yet. Consider how information flows in ways like this when structuring your presentation or document.

You should also consider how you will visually represent the information. In a presentation or document, you can convey information through methods besides text. In fact, if your document only consists of text, it can cause your message to lose its impact or not capture the audience's attention.

For example, if your document has a schedule for an event, consider putting it in a table that has a column for the time slot, the activity, and the presenter. This might convey the information better than a bulleted list.

Speaking of aesthetics, make sure that your presentation or document is appealing. If it is appropriate, feel free to add colors, graphics, icons, and other elements that can make it appear more interesting. You should also pay attention to minor details. For example, is your text consistently sized? Are your paragraphs justified with consistent kerning? Small details like these elevate your presentation or document.

To learn more, I encourage you to read articles about graphic design to learn some more guiding principles. It may even be valuable to learn how to better use Word, PowerPoint, and similar tools.

Building Professional Websites

Today, any business, nonprofit, or even a portfolio needs a website. It is one of the first impressions people will have of you and your work. Thankfully, it's easy to create websites, even if you have no coding or design experience.

It's also cheaper than you might expect. Usually, owning a domain is only $12 per year, and the cost of a website builder typically starts at $15 per month. So, here are some insights that might be helpful to you if you start building one.

The best websites are more than just beautiful (though that is important). The primary purpose of your site is to share information, so you need to outline it in a way that ensures the user can find everything they need to know.

In general, your website should have the following.

- A homepage that provides a high-level overview of the site.
- An about page that goes into more detail about the project, you, and your team.
- A page that goes into more detail about your project, like the services you offer or your service projects.
- A way to contact you or your team (via a contact page, contact form, or listing your email address).
- Links to your social media, if you have any.

Before you start making the website, think about which of these components (and others) should go on your website.

Once you have identified your components, outline the exact information that you will have on each page. Ask yourself if the layout makes sense and delivers information in the best possible way.

Now that you've identified the components and information, start thinking about the design.

First, you should decide how you'll build your website. Are you going to code it yourself, or have someone else do it? Are you going to use a website builder like Wix or Squarespace?

If you've chosen a website builder like Wix, they will have templates for you. Feel free to use one of these templates, expand on it, or start completely from scratch.

I also encourage you to take inspiration from other websites. Design trends are constantly changing, so you can always look to others for examples of ways to improve your site and make a strong impression on your audience.

As a rule of thumb, here are some design considerations you should keep in mind when designing your site.

- Does your website have graphics or images?
- Do you have too much text on pages? Are there giant blocks of text?
- Are you using a consistent color and font scheme across all your pages?
- Is there enough contrast between your text and background?
- Is it easy to find the other pages on your site, links, buttons, and other things users may have to click on?

Helpful Resources

There are many tools, websites, and other resources I've used over the past few years to help me succeed in school and my career.

On the following pages, I've put a list of different resources that might be helpful to you in your journey!

Topic	Resource
Academic Success	**Khanacademy.com** Struggling with a class or topic in school? Check out Khan Academy for instructional videos.
At Home	**Apartmenttherapy.com** Life can be busy, but this is a site for ideas to help clean, decorate, and organize your home. Keep an eye out for their go-to insights on sales and discounts.
Business & Professional Resources	**Linkedin** If you're not on Linkedin yet, you should create a profile ASAP. Nowadays, it's essentially expected that every professional has a Linkedin profile. It's also a tool for networking with others. Be sure to google tips for building a standout Linkedin profile.

Topic	Resource
Business & Professional Resources	**Themuse.com** The Muse has a wide range of articles related to professional development. They also have a job board and place to learn about specific companies.
Business & Professional Resources	Fastcompany.com This is another good website for finding business news and helpful articles to grow your professional skills.
Civic Engagement	**When We All Vote** This organization helps voters get registered, stay up-to-date on their voting status, and learn about their voting rights. Visit their site to learn more and get involved.
Civic Engagement	Icivics.org This site has games to teach you about the different parts of the local, state, and federal government.
College Research	Usnews.com/best-colleges This is a great site for finding information about colleges. It also offers rankings for various categories and insights into different types of majors.
Disinformation & Misinformation	Getbadnews.com This fun, interactive experience shows you how misinformation and disinformation can easily spread and helps you learn how to be more informed yourself.

Topic	Resource
Disinformation & Misinformation	**Allsides.com** This site collects articles about current events from all sides of the political spectrum. This is a way to see what different perspectives are saying and create your own informed opinion.
Diversity & Equity	**Racialequitytools.org** More than ever, it's important for all of us to know and adopt best practices related to diversity, equity, and inclusion. This means in our schools, places of work, community, and personal lives. This website helps you learn the fundamentals and important concepts related to diversity and equity.
Diversity & Equity	**Diversitybestpractices.com** This website provides news, resources, and events to learn more about diversity and equity.
Document Templates	**Canva** Canva has thousands of design templates for all kinds of documents - everything from flyers, to reports, to presentations, and more. Check out Canva to easily create a beautiful document or get inspiration.

Topic	Resource
Entrepreneurship	**Entrepreneur.com** If you're interested in entrepreneurship or business, this website should be a part of your daily reading. It is a place to learn about trends, market news, and more.
Entrepreneurship	**Inc.com** Inc. is a great source for professional, business, and entrepreneurial advice, articles, resources, and more.
Event Management	**Eventbrite.com** If you are ever hosting or managing an event, especially one that requires RSVPs or tickets, Eventbrite is a great and easy tool to use.
Financial Wellness	**Nerdwallet.com** Wanting to get serious about financial wellness? Nerdwallet has great articles and resources for making the best decisions about everything from credit cards, student loans, banking, and more.
Financial Wellness	**Acorns** Investing in your future is important - but it can be hard to set aside money regularly to do it. If this problem sounds familiar to you, check out Acorns. It's a great app that automatically rounds up your purchases and invests the money for you.

Topic	Resource
Financial Wellness	**Grow.acorns.com** Ran by Acorns, Grow has articles on financial wellness and analysis on current events that could affect your money.
Financial Wellness	**Mint** This is one of the most common budgeting and credit monitoring apps out there. Among other things, it allows you to track balances in your accounts, set financial goals, and track bills. Check this out to help you build and follow budgets.
Lifelong Learning	**Grownandflown.com** This site has tons of articles on every topic that high schoolers and college students need to know about. This includes things like academics, relationships, finding the right college, and more.
Lifelong Learning	**Udemy.com** Udemy offers thousands of online courses on almost any topic you can imagine. Whether you want to learn about coding, video production, writing, or anything else, Udemy has you covered.
Lifelong Learning	Classcentral.com This site offers free Ivy League courses on a variety of topics. They are self-paced, so you can learn at your convenience!

Topic	Resource
Mental Health	**Happiful** Happiful has articles about everything from mental health, relationships, overall wellbeing, and more.
Mental Health	**Psychcentral.com** Psych Central teaches you about different mental conditions and takes informative looks at the mental health effects of current events.
News and Podcasts	**NPR.com** If you're looking for news stories about current events, pop culture, or any other type of media, check out NPR. There is a wealth of articles and podcasts you can find.
Nonprofit	**Donorbox.org/nonprofit-blog** For resources on starting a nonprofit, check out this page. It offers advice for everything from starting a nonprofit to fundraising and more.
Nutrition	**Budgetbytes.com** Wanting to cook on a budget? Check out budgetbytes.com for hundreds of delicious, but inexpensive, recipes.
Nutrition	**Fitmencook.com** Don't let the name fool you. This user-friendly site has recipes for anyone looking to eat healthy, but not boring. Kevin Curry is the king of healthy yet fun cooking!

Helpful Resources

Topic	Resource
Physical Health	**My Fitness Pal** This is an app that combines calorie tracking, workout routines, and more in one convenient package.
Physical Health	**Nike Training App** This app has hundreds of workouts you can follow, and it tracks your workouts. It also has cool features, like discounts on Nike products as rewards for working out.
Productive Distractions	**The New York Times Crossword** Need a break but want to train your brain? Check out The New York Time's famous daily crossword.
Productive Distractions	**Lumosity** Work out your brain by checking out Lumosity's huge library of brain games.
Productive Distractions	**Websudoku.com** There are few better ways to train your logic skills than mastering Sudoku. Check it out the next time you're looking for a productive distraction.
Productivity	**Todo.microsoft.com** This is a simple tool for making and organizing to-do lists.

Helpful Resources

Topic	Resource
Productivity	**Google Drive** If you aren't already using Google Drive, then you should check it out ASAP. It has a suite of programs like Docs and Slides that allow for collaboration. Most conveniently, it gives you a centralized place to store all your files. This can help you stay organized and keep records of everything you do. I also love that it autosaves your work!
Productivity	**Grammarly** This is a newer, but very well-regarded tool that can help check your writing for grammar, spelling mistakes, and even consistency and tone.
Service	**Dosomething.org** This site provides ideas for service projects geared towards young people. If you're ever wanting to find ways to serve, this is a great place to start.
Service	**Volunteermatch.com** This site helps you find various service opportunities that may be offered in your area.
Websites	**Google Domains** Looking for a place to buy a domain? One of the best options is Google's Domain services. It allows you to easily purchase a domain.

Topic	Resource
Websites	**Google Workspace** Speaking of Google, this is an important tool if you own a website. This is basically Google Drive, but for your website. This is how you get customized emails (you@yourwebsite.com) and other valuable services for your project. Don't forget to check out their nonprofit pricing.
Websites	**Google Analytics** Another powerful tool for your website is Google Analytics. This lets you access information like how many people visit your site, trends, and other helpful data.
Websites	**Wix** One of the simplest website builders out there, it features a drag-and-drop interface that is easy to use and plenty of templates to get you started.

Glossary

Through my experiences starting a nonprofit and working on entrepreneurial projects, I've learned many useful terms. I wanted to share some terms that I think will be helpful for you to know.

Terms

501(c)(3) Tax-Exempt Status: is a U.S. Internal Revenue Service (IRS) designation nonprofits can apply for. Section 501(c)(3) is the portion of the US Internal Revenue Code that allows for nonprofit organizations to be exempt from taxes. To qualify as a tax-exempt, 501(c)(3) organization, a nonprofit must exist for one or more exclusively charitable purposes: religious, charitable, scientific, testing for public safety, literary, educational, fostering of national or international amateur sports, and prevention of cruelty to animals and children.

Articles of Incorporation: are a set of formal documents filed with a government body to legally document the creation of a corporation or nonprofit. This set of documents generally contain pertinent information such as the firm's name, street address, agent for service of process, and more.

Board of Directors: is the governing body of a company or nonprofit. Individuals who sit on the board are responsible for overseeing the organization's activities. Board members meet periodically to discuss and vote on the affairs of the organization.

Bylaws: are the governing rules by which the organization operates. When an organization is formed, the first act of the board of directors must be to create the bylaws, which is a single document encompassing the rules pertaining to the organization.

Capital: are financial assets an organization has, including equipment, real estate, and anything an organization needs to continue providing goods or services.

Corporate Social Responsibility (CSR): is a self-regulating business model that facilitates companies acting in a socially accountable way. Engaging in this means that a company is operating in ways that positively contribute to society and the environment. This can include a variety of programs such as philanthropy and volunteering, among others.

Credit Union: are not-for-profit organizations that serve their members. Like banks, credit unions accept deposits, make loans and provide financial services. As member-owned and cooperative institutions, credit unions provide a safe place to save and borrow at reasonable rates.

Domain Name: is a unique name that identifies a website. All domain names have a domain suffix, such as .com, .net, or .org. This helps identify the type of website the domain name represents. For example, ".com" domain names are typically used by commercial websites, while ".org" websites are usually used by nonprofits organizations. Domains are generally registered through services like Google Domains or GoDaddy.

Employer Identification Number (EIN): is a number used to identify a business entity or nonprofit. This number is issued by the U.S. Internal Revenue Service (IRS). Every business and nonprofit needs to have one, as it's necessary to do things such as getting a business banking account. This is also known as a Federal Tax Identification Number.

Form 990: is a form used by tax-exempt organizations to provide information to the U.S. Internal Revenue Service (IRS). This public document provides information such as fiscal data for the foundation, names of trustees and officers, application information, and a complete grants list.

Grant: is money provided by an organization to a nonprofit for a specific purpose. This includes scholarships, research grants, funding for community projects, and more.

Human Resources: is the division of a business that finds, hires, and trains job applicants. They also sometimes are responsible for overseeing a company's corporate social responsibility programs.

Impact Report: is a communication strategy used to convey the change created by an organization or activity, and how that change was created. An impact report is not merely a description of the activities affecting change because it also should include analyses about how much difference happened.

In-Kind Donations: are donations of goods, services, or time, but not money. This includes things like equipment, books, cars, advertising, and transportation, among others.

Incubator: is a collaborative program often sponsored by private companies, municipal entities, or public institutions to help create and grow young businesses. They accomplish this by providing them with necessary financial and technical support, as well as expertise. There are many kinds of incubators that serve niches, like technology, nonprofits, diversity initiatives, and more.

Invoice: is a time-stamped record of a transaction between two parties. This includes purchases made by a buyer, but an invoice can also record services that charge an hourly fee and sponsorships. The invoice usually specifies the terms of the deal and provides information on the available methods of payment.

Key Performance Indicator (KPI): is a measurable value that demonstrates how effectively a company is achieving key business objectives. Organizations use KPIs at multiple levels to evaluate their success at reaching targets.

Mission Statement: is a brief description of an entity's fundamental purpose. It answers the question, "Why does our business (or nonprofit or government agency) exist?" The mission statement articulates the company's purpose both for those in the organization and for the public.

Nonprofit Organization: is a business that has been granted tax-exempt status by the Internal Revenue Service (IRS) because it furthers a social cause and provides a public benefit.

Profit: is the income a company or nonprofit has left over after expenses, discounts, and taxes are subtracted from revenue.

Revenue: is the income a company or nonprofit generates before any expenses are taken out.

Search Engine Optimization (SEO): is the process of improving your site to increase its visibility for relevant searches. The better visibility your pages have in search results, the more likely you are to garner attention and attract prospective and existing customers to your business.

Secretary of State: is a position within most states that holds many responsibilities. This includes keeping state records, registering businesses and nonprofits, overseeing elections in the state, certifying documents, and more. This is the office where you would likely register your organization at the state level.

Vision Statement: is a sentence or short paragraph that succinctly describes the goals of a company, nonprofit, or some other entity. It states what you are trying to build and serves as a touchstone for your future actions. Unlike a mission statement, this is usually an internal statement that describes the future of the organization, not what it currently does.

W-9: is an Internal Revenue Service (IRS) tax form that is used to confirm a person's name, address, and taxpayer identification number (TIN). Generally, this form is used in employment or any time a payment is being made (e.g. a sale, sponsorship).

Sources

These terms were sourced from the following organizations.

- Ballotpedia
- Candid
- Entrepreneur
- Foundation Group
- Investopedia
- IRS
- Klipfolio
- MissionBox
- MyCreditUnion.gov
- Oxford Languages
- Search Engine Land
- Sopact
- Tech Terms
- The Balance Small Business

Made in the USA
Columbia, SC
13 April 2022

58934271R00105